10 PRINCIPLES OF
ARTFUL GARDEN DESIGN

10 GARDEN DESIGN PRINCIPLES

SUSIE WHITE

VIVAYS PUBLISHING

Published by Vivays Publishing Ltd
www.vivays-publishing.com

A catalogue record for this book is available
from the British Library

ISBN 978-1-908126-32-0
Publishing Director: Lee Ripley
Designer: Draught Associates

Cover: Getty Images/Relaxfoto.de
Frontispiece: GAP Photos/ Andrea Jones

Printed in China

CONTENTS

INTRODUCTION

INTRODUCTION

Garden design is an art form though it often isn't recognised as such. It is not ranked in the same way as painting or sculpture yet its best examples transcend everyday reality. A garden can challenge, delight and remain in the memory as much as a visit to a gallery. The design of a garden requires imagination and creativity and deals with much the same elements as the visual arts: form, colour, texture, line, scale and composition. Yet a garden is more than a visual art, it can stimulate all five senses.

I have gardened all my life, from my earliest endeavors with a child's wheelbarrow, struggling to dig with an oversized garden fork. In the garden of my childhood it was the rough edges that most inspired me, the wild plants that frothed under orchard trees or grew without design in neglected corners.

LEFT
Plants flow in a seemingly natural way in Susie's garden

PREVIOUS PAGE
Art and gardening meet in Monet's water garden at Giverny

As an adult, I drew on these childhood memories for Chesters Walled Garden that I opened next to Hadrian's Wall in northern England—now sadly closed after 23 years. From my work there, I gained in confidence as I developed my own style, a mix of topiary, wildflowers and perennials.

Now with a private garden I am able to experiment, planting without constraints. It is exciting to have bare ground onto which I can daub colours and let my imagination go. There are many approaches to designing an artful garden. One approach is freeform, impressionistic, abstract, going on instinct as to which plants feel right next to each other. This is not the only way though. Like a painting, a garden can be meticulously planned, its preliminary drawings carefully followed and executed. Whatever approach you take, however, should feel exuberant and fun.

I trained in fine art at the Ruskin School of Drawing in Oxford, established by John Ruskin, the great thinker, reformer, artist and gardener of the nineteenth century. Ruskin's garden at Brantwood on the side of Coniston Water in the English Lake District is an inspiring place where the sustainability, local materials and intellectual ideas that he believed in are still being tried out. He advocated direct observation of nature; it is through observation of plants that we can best understand where and how to grow them. As an art student at Ruskin's school, I would spend hours in the Oxford Botanic Garden, drawing in the exotic glasshouses or learning about plant families from the order beds.

Just across the road is Magdalen College where the river meadows in spring are famous for their profusion of snake's head fritillaries. These exquisite and rare wildflowers are dusky jewels with chequered purple or white nodding bells. This timeless meadow, studded like a medieval flowery mead, became added to my memory of childhood plants, along with visits to famous gardens such as Hidcote Manor in Gloucestershire. Then, when I moved to the north of England, I discovered the upland hay meadows of the North Pennines, rich in biodiversity, colourful and flowing in their undulating lines. All these influences were thrown into the pot and my gardening style evolved, in tune with the New Naturalism movement, which also draws on natural or farmed landscapes.

Nodding flowers of snake's head fritillary *Fritillaria meleagris* in Magdalen Meadow, Oxford, England

My challenge with this new garden has been to make it fit with the surrounding landscape. Set in a quiet valley, bounded by river and stream, with views to low hills and native trees, it references the colours, shapes and patterns of the valley meadows, the wild grassy slopes. It has been exhilarating to paint with plants, laying them on the soil without a detailed plan, but there have been two guiding themes: one to do with colour, one seasonal.

To extend the sense of space across what is a large rectangle, hot colours are grouped closest to the house, cool colours positioned further away. As cool colours appear to recede and warm colours to come closer, this makes the garden appear larger than it is, as well as allowing the softer hues to blend with rather than jar against the fields beyond. The second theme utilises time. Spring begins under the shelter of a line of trees on the west side before flowing across the garden to the east where it culminates in late flowering perennials and grasses. So the garden acts as a large calendar, tracing the time through the year across the background canvas that is the soil.

Time is the extra dimension that makes gardening so thrilling and so difficult. Plants rise and fall in height, move, change, mature, die back, so the relationship between them is constantly shifting. This is what makes the novice gardener so unsure about how to put them together. One way to learn is to take inspiration from the unselfconscious layout of the cottage garden and simply try things out. Enjoy the way that plants are constantly changing as the year ebbs and flows. The gardening year is a cycle and it is hard to know where it begins and ends. The fact that it is not static but is constantly on the move creates great challenges; one moment it can be a masterpiece, the next it falls from grace. Juggling all these changeable elements is the essence of the craft of gardening.

ABOVE
Romantic planting in the Gertrude Jekyll garden, Upton Grey, Hampshire, England

RIGHT
Gravetye Manor, England, home of the original 'wild gardener' William Robinson

The naturalistic style of making gardens is as relevant to urban areas as it is to rural, and brings a sense of a wider landscape to our cities. The New Perennial movement began in Europe in the 1990s and uses swathes of perennials that can happily co-exist in a seemingly natural and flowing design. These ideas can be traced back to the nineteenth century and the work of Irishman William Robinson and his seminal book *The Wild Garden*. Reacting against the formality and wastefulness of Victorian bedding schemes, his gardens of hardy perennials and native plants paralleled the British Arts and Crafts movement. The great plantswoman Gertrude Jekyll contributed to his magazine *The Garden* and their garden collaborations and friendship lasted for over 50 years.

Mien Ruys, whose father was a friend to Jekyll, experimented with planting combinations on the family nursery at Moerheim in the Netherlands, where in the twentieth century she created a series of 25 model gardens. She believed in adapting plants to their site and her designs were characterised by blocks of hedges on different levels, their formality softened by grasses, perennials, bulbs and water. Together with Piet Oudolf, she is hailed as a leader of the New Perennial movement, a movement which has resonated worldwide and is now much utilised in the large scale planting of parks and urban spaces.

City designs often need to adapt to limited soils and challenging sites. Piet Oudolf was commissioned to transform the High Line, an elevated, abandoned freight line running high among the buildings of New York's West Side. Now a linear public park, its naturalistic plantings echo the self-seeded wildness that once grew between the disused tracks. It is an example of a style that finds its inspiration in the natural environment, as does the New American Garden movement seen in the work of Oehme, van Sweden and Associates from Washington DC. Drawing on the great sweeps and colours of the prairies, this approach interweaves tough, reliable, native American flowers with ornamental grasses for their year round qualities. There is an appreciation of plants even in decay, of seed heads left to stand amongst the swaying mass.

ABOVE
Subtle planting on New York's High Line emulates natural landscapes

LEFT
Layers of hedges in Mien Ruys' garden in the Netherlands

Artfully simple planting in Schupf garden designed by Oehme, van Sweden and Associates, New York State

Since the 1990s the New Perennial movement has been absorbed into popular gardening in the same way that the catwalks influence high street design. It fits in with an awareness of the fragility of ecosystems and the importance of native plants. With its emphasis on choosing the right plant for the right place, this style is adaptable to different countries where local distinctiveness can be shown in the selection of native wildflowers. It generally employs a fairly limited, harmonious palette of purples, reds, browns and yellows.

The opposite of this is the highly coloured grouping of exotic plants, with late season dahlias and cannas jostling with the sculptural leaves of banana plants and palms. Very suitable for the small town garden, this style is strong on foliage as well as brilliant in colour. It can create a fantasy space, a world within a world, an escape from everyday reality. Compared to the washes of colour of the New Perennial movement, it has the strength and decorative rhythms of a Rousseau painting.

In this book I will show the ten key principles of designing an artful garden. While the words that constantly emerge are words that are also applied to the visual arts such as colour and form, as well as the more subtle facets such as layers and light, there is much more to a garden. Unlike a painting, the garden is a living artwork and the plants grow and fade, changing with the seasons as well as over time, adding another dimension to the elements that make up artful gardening.

PRINCIPLE 1
COMPOSITION

PRINCIPLE 1
COMPOSITION

Many of the terms used to describe the process of garden design are also terms used by painters. One that has particular resonance with the visual arts is composition. For the designer this has a dual aspect: the bird's eye view of the composition as drawn to scale on paper, as well as how it will appear from the ground, which is an entirely different matter. The flat blueprint has to be imagined as a space to look at and walk through, something that comes largely with experience. The shapes on the plan become altered by perspective and the planting will be three-dimensional not two.

Creating the pattern

The design on paper is essentially a pattern, one that benefits from balance. Most people use the house as a fixed starting point from which to work out the boundaries. Once this is drawn to scale, the fun can start. It's a good idea to print off multiple sheets of the outline so that you can play around with ideas without constraint, drawing rectangles, circles, triangles, curves or abstract shapes. Once these main blocks create a satisfying pattern, you can then start to think about how they might translate into separate areas of use and interest. With a strong, underlying design a garden has unity; the surface textures of planting, materials, furniture and water are then added to this base.

With the composition having much in common with art it is no surprise that gardeners often look to paintings for inspiration. The Dutch painter Mondrian was a master of the division of space with his grid-based paintings using blocks of primary colours and white spaces. Mondrian was one of the influences on the Lawleys' layout for Herterton House in northern England. It is the juxtaposition of weight and balance which makes Mondrian's work so applicable to garden plans, his blocks of colour being readily translated into areas of paving or the mass of colour that is the planting.

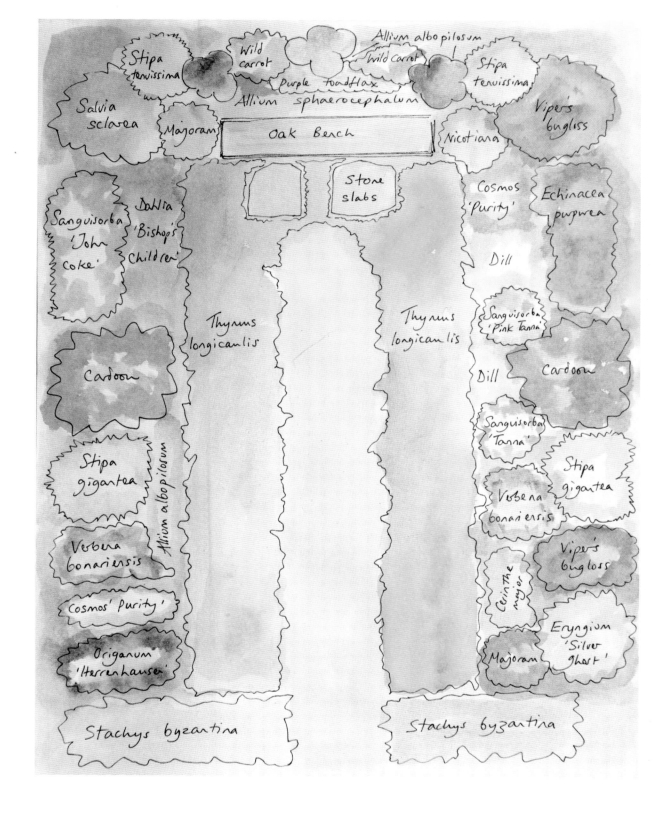

Stipa tenuissima

Wild carrot

Allium albopilosum

Wild carrot

Stipa tenuissima

Salvia sclarea

Majoram

Purple toadflax

Allium sphaerocephalum

Oak Bench

Nicotiana

Viper's bugloss

Stone slabs

Cosmos 'Purity'

Echinacea purpurea

Sanguisorba 'John coke'

Dahlia 'Bishop's Children'

Dill

Thymus longicaulis

Thymus longicaulis

Sanguisorba 'Pink Tanna'

Cardoon

Dill

Cardoon

Sanguisorba 'Tanna'

Stipa gigantea

Allium albopilosum

Stipa gigantea

Verbena bonariensis

Verbena bonariensis

Viper's bugloss

Cerinthe major

Cosmos 'Purity'

Origanum 'Herrenhausen'

Majoram

Eryngium 'Silver Ghost'

Stachys byzantina

Stachys byzantina

A painterly garden - Herterton House
in Northumberland, England

Minimalist planting seen through a purple wall Texas, USA

Geometric shapes

Squares and circles, circles within squares and other geometric shapes underpinning the garden bring a feeling of calm. Translated into reality they create lines of sight altered by perspective: the narrowing view down a path, the squashed oval shape of a pool that was a circle when drawn on the plan. The planting can echo the composition of this design with the equilibrium of topiary, trees or objects on either side of the main lines of sight. This geometry and balance can work for formal gardens as well as minimalist spaces with their simple, clean lines, reduced colour palette and limited number of materials as well as lack of ornamentation. Gardens work well if they reflect the architecture of the buildings that they surround. The minimalist garden that uses strong shapes is the perfect match for modern architecture.

Curves and freeform shapes

Dividing up the garden space need not rely on geometric
shapes. Fluid lines, curves and freeform shapes bring
movement and dynamic quality to the design. The American
artist and garden designer, Topher Delaney, specialises
in healing gardens. In her design for San Diego Children's
Hospital, brightly coloured walls form arcs that partly enclose
a lively and fun play area. A delightful touch is the use of light
and shadow in the form of animal shapes pierced through the
walls. The confident curves of the walls with their energetic
colours make a backdrop for simple planting: yellow daisies
like those in a child's drawing, grey eucalyptus trunks, spikes
of scented lavender.

**Exuberant strong colours in
San Diego Children's Hospital
garden, USA**

ABOVE
Asymmetric balance comes from
careful positioning, Santa Barbara,
USA

RIGHT
Symmetric balance lends a calm
to this elegant doorway

Creating a visual balance

Symmetry and asymmetry evoke different reactions as we
move through the garden space. Symmetry can give a sense
of order and calm, though if not well thought out it can be
predictable and dull. With its identical pairs of elements and
its classic design, symmetry can be copied from inspirational
gardens and may often be the choice of the novice designer.
Asymmetry relies equally on a sense of balance: a balance
of interest as well as of weight. To create visual balance and
equilibrium it is necessary to put what may be very different
elements into the composition in a way that retains stability.

Using the rule of thirds is a helpful tool in achieving
balance and harmony in the garden. This is an idea that is very
familiar to painters and photographers, in which rectilinear
space is divided by two lines horizontally and two lines
vertically. The subdivisions created are nine equal rectangles.
The four intersections are known as 'power points' and by
placing an object on one of these points the composition is
pleasing to the eye. The rule of thirds may be used in the
ground plan of a design or in an artfully framed view. Although
our angle of sight varies as we walk around a garden, the view
through a doorway or window can be composed to present
a set piece. In the photograph on page 32, looking out to the
mountains, the American designer Steve Martino has framed
the Arizona landscape beyond the low wall of the patio through
the open doors. It is at these points of entry and exit that the
view can be most directly controlled. Looking through a wall
into another part of the garden, what we see is framed for us
and we see it as the designer intended.

Steve Martino garden in Arizona
with view of mountains

Zen and the art of garden design

Japanese Shunmyo Masuno is an eighteenth generation Zen priest and the last of his order still involved in making gardens. The serene oases that he creates are in the heart of the modern cities of Tokyo and Yokohama. He sees it as his responsibility to help people to rediscover their humanity through the carefully composed gardens that he makes in the Japanese and Buddhist traditions. Looking at how it suggests itself to be sited, Masuno has placed each rock according to its nature. These gardens are rich in metaphor; a sleek upright rock represents a fish attempting to leap the obstacle of a waterfall, encouraging the viewer to overcome their own obstacles and challenges.

Masuno designed a wave garden for the Cerulean Tower Hotel in Tokyo using huge blocks of stone, great sweeping curves of quarried ledges, planted between with mosses, ferns and evergreen shrubs. This is designed to be seen from within the hotel, like most of his gardens, rather than walked in. The result is a series of compositions framed within the edges of plate glass windows. We are able to view them devoid of moving figures. Masuno describes the garden as a spiritual place in which the mind dwells and sees the act of its creation as part of his quest for a higher understanding of himself.

PRINCIPLE 2
SIZE AND SCALE

PRINCIPLE 2
SIZE AND SCALE

For centuries, artists have distorted scale to produce an emotional response, whether in religious paintings or in Surrealist art. By making a leap in scale, painters and sculptors have revealed the new. Taking an everyday object and blowing it up in size transforms it into something extraordinary seen with fresh eyes. A reduction in size has a different effect; think of how we marvel at the beauty of a Nicholas Hilliard miniature. In the same way in gardens, unusual or unexpected scale can be an attention grabber and can overturn our expectations about how a space might be filled.

LEFT
Lush greenery creates an oasis in this town garden, Brighton, England

PREVIOUS PAGE
Careful design has made this narrow London garden appear spacious

A circular lawn gives this small garden a feeling of width

Playing with size

Playing with size in proportion to setting is yet another way that gardeners can create mood. At Hidcote Manor in Gloucestershire, England, Major Lawrence Johnston made a huge, circular, raised bathing pool that almost completely fills a hedged enclosure. Walking into this garden compartment, dominated by its sheet of still water, you are acutely aware of the water and the sides of the tall, dark hedge. The scale of the pool to its surroundings evokes a completely different feeling to the more usual size of a pond in a garden 'room'.

Filling a small, square back garden with a large circular lawn has the same effect as the bathing pool at Hidcote. It pushes back the boundaries giving a greater sense of width. The points of a diamond also appear to push back the fence line and by disguising the perimeters and blurring them with climbing plants the garden feels larger still. Vertical height is also important, with trees and pergolas lifting the eye up. Simplifying paving materials and keeping them to the same colours as the house also increases scale.

In the restricted space of a small urban yard an artfully placed group of a few very large pots creates far more effect than lots of little ones. In the ground planting of a small area,

the repetition of a few key varieties, rather than diminishing the scale, makes the garden feel larger. It is all too easy to be seduced by plants in flower at the garden centre and to buy on impulse something that later gets lost amongst all the others. By mass planting and limiting the colours to perhaps three you can use the simplicity of just a few varieties to increase the garden's apparent size.

A trick that designers often employ is to increase the feeling of size in a garden by using mirrors. Particularly in town courtyard gardens with their high walls and limited space, a mirror can give the illusion of a continuing path, of a window or a door into a second garden. This adds depth and accentuates light, doubling the number of plants and creating another world beyond this one. It is such a simple technique but very effective. Even though we know it is illusory, it still produces a sense of increased space. A mirror can even be placed beyond a door that is ajar, teasingly inviting us to open the door onto a further garden. Water too can act like a mirror, increasing the apparent openness of an area, reflecting sky and buildings, as seen in the Berlin town garden pictured above. Like a horizontal mirror it replicates any plants on its margins.

Altered perspective

In this Dublin garden, the repetition of foliage shapes, the softening of the boundaries with tall plants and a path leading into the greenery, its end lost from sight, all serve to increase the sense of scale as well as adding mystery. A real sense of drama can be created by growing exotic plants in an urban garden, the glossy greens and strong foliage patterns turning it into a private world. By placing large plants in front, the depth of the garden can be increased. The same art is employed in Japanese gardens where, to create an illusion of greater size, larger groups of rocks are positioned in the foreground and smaller trees are planted in the distance. This is known as altered perspective.

Playing with scale

Garden design can manipulate scale, using large shapes in unexpected ways. This can create an Alice-in-Wonderland-like fantasy or echo Surrealist painting. A garden can become a dreamlike space that plays with scale, featuring distortions, visual puns and mysterious shapes where the usual 'rules' of scale are suspended. The extraordinary Surrealist fantasy garden of Laz Posas in Mexico completely distorts any normal sense of scale. In this tropical mountain landscape with its nine pools fed by waterfalls, the eccentric millionaire Edward James created 36 reinforced concrete structures between the early 1960s and his death in 1984. Amongst these dreamlike constructions, two of his sculptures stand at over 6 metres (approx 20 feet) in height, towering into the verdant jungle. A stairway to nowhere spirals into the sky. A pair of hands emerges from the foliage. It is unsettling, fantastical and totally unique.

Tiny alpine plants in a brick trough

The size of plants provokes an emotional response. There is a delicate vulnerability about tiny specimens growing in an alpine trough. Exhibits at alpine shows are crowded with people admiring the rows of terracotta pans, their plants teased to perfection with tweezers, not a leaf out of place. There is beauty in the fragility of the small. In the opposite way, when plants loom above our heads the scale is altered so that we become small ourselves, rekindling childhood memories. By planting tall waving grasses, asters, cardoons and giant thistles that we have to look up at to admire, we evoke those days when we were smaller. It is not just about the size of plants in relation to each other, but also about their size compared to us. Changing size and scale in the garden becomes something we can play with to evoke memory and feeling.

Getting the proportions right

When size and scale are in proportion in the garden there is a rightness to things. This is especially true in the use of materials. The size of paving slabs need to be in the right ratio for the house, the width of a path the appropriate scale for its surroundings, a summerhouse a suitable size for the terrace it sits on. Knowing what is fitting is about a sensitivity to the place. Even the right size of gravel can matter. Of course, like any set of rules, the confident designer can go in completely the opposite direction, making a tiny, thin path through a large green space or setting a monolithic stone bench in a small garden. Size and scale are there to be conformed to - or to play with and distort like Alice following the directions on the bottle!

Clusters of terracotta pots on paving in an Italian style garden in Bavaria

PRINCIPLE 3
LINE, PATTERN
AND SHAPE

PRINCIPLE 3
LINE, PATTERN AND SHAPE

Line is everywhere in the garden, from the mid rib of a leaf to the edge of a garden path. Described in the dictionary as the identifiable path of a moving point, it is something to be cleverly used in leading the eye through the spaces of the garden.

Line can be straight, curved, serpentine, squiggly, spiralling, vertical, horizontal or diagonal; it can go in any direction and be varied in width or length. It can divide up the space as well as enclose it and define it. Line can be calming and serene, evoking a sense of peace, or as meandering and crazy as the surface of a Jackson Pollock painting.

And when lines, be they wavy or straight, are repeated they can transform the green space of a lawn as they curve into the distance. It is with this repetition that line becomes pattern. Pattern is the repetition of shapes and lines.

Wavy lines in lawn

LEFT
Formal garden at Herterton House

PREVIOUS PAGE
Glorious pattern comes from farming lavender

The lines of this path appear to narrow due to perspective

Line and perspective

Wherever we stand in a garden, we see it before us in two dimensions, as if in a painting; this is when we are most acutely aware of the lines laid out in front of us.

The parallel lines of a path, which can direct the eye to a focal point, are often used by garden designers to lead to a sculpture, bench or other 'full stop' of an object. There is an integrity and honesty about a straight path leading to a front door; flanked by aromatic lavender bushes it is friendly and welcoming. Perspective appears to bring parallel lines together; this draws the visitor enticingly down the garden path. Playing with that perspective can alter the appearance of the scale of the space in front. By narrowing the path as it travels away from the viewer, the garden can appear larger than it actually is. Widening the path at its end has the effect of foreshortening it.

Perspective can be played around with when planting avenues of trees or designing with water. At Blagdon Hall in Northumberland, England, Sir Edwin Lutyens designed a 'sky-mirror' canal when he redesigned parts of the garden in 1938. Nearly two hundred metres long, it employs perspective to give a greater sense of length by tapering its distant sides. In the French formal gardens of the seventeenth century, the same technique was used on allées and lines of trees; they were planted so that they converged in the distance or pruned so that they became shorter as they retreated from the viewer.

Whole treatises were written about bending the rules of perspective in creating these tree-lined avenues.

Such lines are particularly strong in the geometric layouts of classic formality. In the gardens of the English Arts and Crafts movement, designers such as Lutyens and Jekyll arrived at a pleasing synthesis between formality and informality. The strict lines are still there underlying the garden but there is a wilder froth of planting, softening and disguising the layout. Plants are allowed to flop over the sides of the path but the edges are still seen in places, leading the eye to the end point. This style has been copied endlessly since the Edwardian period and is still much loved because of its blend of the formal and the informal, of constraint and freedom.

In the New Perennial movement the lines of paths are often done away with entirely so that the view of a walk through the planting is suggested rather than delineated. This is helped by the extensive use of gravel as a weed suppressant and moisture retainer. Used to top the borders as well, the gravel makes a seamless flow between the plants and the walk, so that the path is hinted at purely by the lack of planting along its length. The eye is coaxed very softly along the view, resting every now and then on the grasses or perennials that almost meet in the middle. This is a pathway

TOP
Lutyens and Jekyll worked together on Hestercombe Gardens, Somerset, England

BOTTOM
A path is suggested rather than delineated in this gravel garden

that may lead in a straight line or meander through the fulsomeness of a meadow.

As well as lines on the ground, there are vertical lines that can lead the eye upwards. The eye travels across the mass of planting to be met by vertical shapes that it then ascends, creating a visual dynamism and excitement. Using verticals in this way brings movement into our picture of the garden. Curved lines also express movement as in the pebble-lined rill that snakes across a wide area know as the Broadwalk in the National Botanic Garden of Wales. Inspired by the meandering course of the nearby River Tywi, its long, slow curves appear to twist faster as it flows away from you, compressed by the perspective of distance.

Line encourages us to walk through a space, giving direction and leading us on. It can be used to dictate the way that we want people to experience the garden. Straight lines give a sense of order, balanced by symmetrically laid out borders. The curved lines of island beds can seem artificial if they are not carefully designed. Undulating lines edging lawns and flower beds can trace shapes around the trunks of trees or rocks, echoing the underlying landscape.

Undulating lines can also be found in a quirky English, vernacular wall known as a crinkle-crankle. This idiosyncratic design was built from the eighteenth century onwards to maximise sun and shelter in walled gardens. Its wavy shape gave it added strength making it a useful design in areas of high winds and avoiding the need for buttressing. At the University of Virginia, USA, there is a series of crinkle-crankle walls designed by Thomas Jefferson. Despite their twists and turns, they use fewer bricks than a conventional

Fibonacci spiral seen in woolly thistle,
Cirsium eriopherum

wall because the serpentine design allows the wall to be built just one brick thick.

Pattern

Exuberant and joyous, pattern occurs throughout nature. Following a mathematical sequence, the beautiful Fibonacci spiral can be seen in the crook of an expanding fern, the complex design of the head of a sunflower, in the fruit spouts of a pineapple. Look closely at many flowers and leaves and you see the serenity of symmetry in the predictable patterns of nature. What we see and marvel at in the natural forms of plants can then be added to by what we create and the way in which we organise and design the garden space.

Pattern can be found in agriculture or in the vegetable garden where plants are grown in easily worked rows. This functional aspect of growing can result in some amazing patterns such as the lines of wheat in a field that curve with the contours of the land. The uniform rows of field-grown lavender are there to make harvesting by machine possible, but when in full and glorious flower they bathe the eye in purple. Their rounded, pruned shapes create very simple, linear patterns that stretch to the horizon. The mass planting

Potager garden

Pristine geometry in the Potager at Villandry, France

of a single species creates a mood through pattern; it can be stimulating, calm, arresting, dynamic or restful.

It is the same in the vegetable garden where pattern is born out of the necessity for regular rows. The different colours and shapes of leaves or stems, the heights of plants, as well as the spaces in between, create attractive patterns that can be taken one step further by the creation of a potager. A French term for an ornamental vegetable garden, it has its origins in the gardens of the French Renaissance which turned the growing of food into high art. To make this functional space more aesthetically pleasing, flowers are grown alongside vegetables, which in turn are chosen for their most colourful, attractive varieties. Geometric beds divide up the plot, their formality adding to the strong design.

The laying out of geometric beds on the earth originated in the knot gardens of the European medieval period. Designed to be seen from the upper windows of the house, and usually made of square compartments, the knot garden consisted of intertwined, low hedges made from herbs: lavender, hyssop, wall germander, thyme, cotton lavender or rosemary, all highly scented as well as useful for the still room where cosmetics and medicines were made. Like the intricate patterns in lace, knot gardens were inspired by English

Tulips and forget-me-nots fill this box parterre

TOP LEFT
Filoli in California

ABOVE
Parterre garden with clipped Berberis at Abbey house gardens, Malmesbury, England

needlework patterns. They were so called because their hedges often appeared to overlap one another.

Filling the spaces with coloured gravel or sand further enhanced the patterns of knot gardens; they were then known as open knots. When in-filled with herbs and flowers, they were called closed knots. A modern and particularly fine example of an open knot garden was made in 1976 at Filoli in California, USA, where the contrasting colours and texture of foliage and the way that some hedges appear to lie over others gives the knot garden a sensuous, sculptural quality.

The parterre evolved from the knot garden, the word derived from the French literally meaning 'on the ground'. Often on a grand scale, it was made from clipped box rather than herbs and these highly elaborate, scrolling designs graced the terraces of European palaces. Victorian garden designers such as the architect Reginald Blomfield, author of *The Formal Garden in England*, laid out parterres along with beds of roses in decorative ornament across the flat ground of terraces. Blomfield's interest in pattern had practical aspects too - he was also the designer of the steel lattice electricity pylon!

ABOVE
Clipped silver mounds of santolina
at Ham House, Surrey, England

RIGHT
William Robinson's garden at Gravetye
Manor, England

The enduring green of box was not the only choice plant for parterres. At Ham House in Surrey, England, is a stunning example of the use of cotton lavender, its silver foliage clipped into perfect domes in a matrix of design and its regular formation punctuated by cones of box. The gardens here were restored by the National Trust in 1975 to their original seventeenth century design by John Smithson and the grey mounds, accentuated by their shadows, have the regularity of fish scales in their exuberant arrangement.

Victorian carpet bedding, of the kind reacted against by William Robinson with his wild gardening style, but promoted by Blomfield, was a further development of the knot garden and the parterre. This used bedding plants - annuals along with tender and exotic plants - grown in hot houses and planted out at no small expense. With its high colour and intricate patterns, it was a style particularly popular in public parks and continued to be so into the twentieth century. Many a town would have complex pictures laid out with bedding plants, often on banks where they could be seen to advantage. Symbols, text, coats of arms, clocks and images of every description could be depicted in thousands of small, highly coloured plants, rigorously pruned to maintain evenness of height. They reflected civic pride, often spelling out the name of the town or even the railway station, a favourite place for sloping banks of coloured bedding.

Gardens of Cragside from National Trust site

Fewer public gardens do this nowadays because of the high cost but at the National Trust house of Cragside in northern England carpet bedding patterns are still created using thousands of colourful plants. It's entirely appropriate to its setting in the Formal Garden, a series of terraces within a Victorian walled garden. Every year the swirling patterns are changed, created from fleshy, grey echevarias, gold pyrethrums, silver antennarias and pink sedums. This example of high Victoriana is set on a long sloping bank in the garden that belonged to Lord Armstrong, whose mansion on its rocky outcrop was the first house in the world to be lit by electricity.

A modern take on carpet bedding is laid out to outstanding success at Waddesdon Manor in Buckinghamshire, England. Thanks to a high-tech system now used by town councils, computers can generate the complex plans that would have taken many more hours to do by hand. Designs can be scanned in before being translated into a grid, the resulting template providing the key to numbers and colours of plants. This frees up the design to allow for flowing creativity, one year created by fashion designer Oscar de la Renta in watercolour-like swathes, another inspired by the changing light in a nearby pool. Some 200,000 bedding plants may be grown to provide these quite extraordinary shows of pattern.

Topiary in particular lends itself to pattern, and
contemporary gardeners are having fun in re-interpreting the
themes of parterres. At Bourton House Garden in the English
Cotswolds, twists of yew and box are meticulously clipped into
swirling, rounded ropes curling against a background of pale
gravel. They circle round and rise to a spiral cone like whipped
cream on top of a scone. These are set off by cake-like slices
of topiary and upright shapes for height. It is playful and
exuberant, literally a new twist on a classic pattern.

Coils of box in contemporary topiary at Bourton House Garden, Cotswolds, England

PRINCIPLE 4
LIGHT

PRINCIPLE 4
LIGHT

Walk in a garden at dawn when light is just beginning to filter in and it will be an entirely different experience from the same garden at bright midday. Different again will be an evening stroll when shadows lengthen and plants are backlit by the retreating sun. On a dull day the garden can be dispiriting and grey; on a clear winter's day it can sparkle with frost. Changing diurnally as well as with the seasons, the qualities of light can evoke such contrary feelings. To the artful gardener this is something to be harnessed, and an awareness of where light falls can contribute hugely to the impact and mood of a garden.

PREVIOUS PAGE
Light floods this coastal garden, La Cervara, Portofino, Italy

LEFT
Early light comes softly through an avenue of trees

North or south facing?

One of the first observations that a garden designer will make when seeing a new space is its aspect. Whether a garden faces north or south will influence not only what plant needs to go where but also the placing of those plants according to where the light will fall. It will also influence the colours used. In areas of clear, saturated sunlight – the Mediterranean for example – strong colour is needed because pastels can look wishy-washy under direct glare. The cooler blues of the palette can look flat and grey. In northern Europe, where the light is gentler and subtler, harmonious colours can be used with abandon, their softer hues not diminished by brilliant light.

The advice often given to a gardener starting out on a new plot is to experience it at various times of the day: to discover the areas of light and shade, the places to enjoy sitting. Sensitivity to the character of light in that particular place can be used to inform the position of objects and the planting scheme. Noticing how shadows fall differently on diverse surfaces may decide what kind of materials to use. For example, when making a gravel path, there are many types of gravel, some rounded from the effects of rivers, some jagged from quarrying, each having different qualities when light falls on them. Larger stones will create multiple shadows; self-binding gravel, which has a high clay content, will appear smooth and allow shadows to lie peacefully across its surface.

ABOVE
Hot colours under strong light - geraniums on a wall in Andalucia, Spain

LEFT
Soft colours suit the light in northern Europe

Serenity in a courtyard garden of the Alhambra, Granada, Spain

Harnessing light and shadow

Larger gardens where there is space for a series of 'garden rooms' can harness the effects of light in each according to their size and the height of perimeter planting. Tall hedges elicit a sense of enclosure, narrowing the light and creating areas of shade. More open enclosures allow the sun to flood in. The emotions evoked by walking between one compartment and another will be different. Wandering through the linked courtyards and gardens of the Alhambra in Granada, Spain, is a superlative, sensuous experience. The physicality of moving from bright light to cool shade is created by the dimensions of each courtyard, often linked by passageways, by the openness of one, the pillared colonnades of another. Water, so important in Islamic gardens, reflects light which ripples across the beautifully carved filigree work in stone.

The Alhambra represents 'paradise on earth' with its division of space by walls, with its theme of water in canals, pools and fountains. The derivation of the word 'paradise' is from old Persian meaning a walled-in garden. The Islamic garden, a calm retreat from an arid landscape, has a serene geometry divided by water channels, a place of scent, colour, light and shade.

This sensual aspect of a garden, which uses light to create mood, is a facet of designing that is often overlooked. Perhaps this is because it takes time to observe the results of daily changes. Once you notice that a plant harnesses light in a particular position, then you can repeat its planting to maximise the effect. Purple and red foliage takes on a jewel-like intensity with low evening light. The backlit leaves of the smoke bush, *Cotinus coggyria*, the ruby red mid ribs of bloody sorrel, corrugated, purple rhubarb leaves and burgundy foliage of elephant's ears become radiant as the sun transforms them.

Jewel colours are revealed as low sun illuminates these ruby chard leaves

Shadows add another dimension to this hornbeam walk

Evening light shines behind grasses in the author's garden

This transformation is what professional garden photographers try to capture by working at sunrise and sunset. The light is too strong in the middle of the day, ironing out colours to make them flat and lifeless. But at the opposite ends of day the low angle of the sun illuminates plants showing off every tiny hair on a stem, every vein in a leaf. Grasses look particularly fine with the light glittering on their seed heads in autumn and winter. An observation of this can inform where to position them so that this dazzling effect can be seen from a bench or from house windows. Thinking about where shadows lie can also influence where to plant trees or place topiary. Shadows create striations across a lawn cast by regularly spaced trunks of trees. A topiary shape can act as a sundial giving a sense of the passage of time throughout the day.

Using artificial light

The moon casts shadows too, but often it is impossible to see this subtle effect because of light pollution. Using artificial light creates a different kind of magic, recasting the garden as a dramatic space, revealing things about it that are not seen by day. Uplighters reveal every texture on silver birch stems, strings of lights sparkle amongst clipped box domes, water takes on an otherworldly mood and candles flicker in glass containers. The garden becomes a performance space, a theatre set waiting for something to happen. The garden lit up completely changes the experience of it from that of daylight. Roof gardens in urban areas can make full use of lighting to create places to eat outside. Unlike sunlight, the gardener can choose exactly which parts to illuminate, pinpointing specimen plants, sending beams of light up into trees, making a water feature flow and come to life. The designer has complete control, the opposite to natural lighting and weather.

An urban garden lit up at night becomes a magical space

PRINCIPLE 5
COLOUR

PRINCIPLE 5
COLOUR

Colour makes the garden come truly alive. With an entire palette to choose from, it can be stimulating, vibrant and enlivening or calming, harmonious and understated. It is found not only in flowers but also in leaves, stems, fruits, seeds and bark. It can be applied to materials, furniture and buildings. It changes with the light, the seasons, the time of day, but above all, colour creates mood and elicits emotion.

Artists are familiar with the colour wheel, a depiction of colours laid out in a circle showing their relationship to each other. The primary colours, red, yellow and blue, are pure colours, not created by mixing with any other colours. These are arranged around the circle with the secondaries of the traditional artist's palette set in between them: orange, green and purple. There are also six tertiary colours, more subtle variations, such as red-orange, yellow-orange and so on. These are made by mixing a primary and a secondary together. It was the German artist, writer and polymath Goethe who created the symmetric six-colour wheel for his book *Theory of Colour* and it influenced painters such as Turner and, later, Kandinsky.

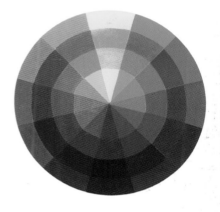

Colour wheel illustration

LEFT
Masterful planting in this apricot and yellow scheme

PREVIOUS PAGE
Field of gold - a path threads through a meadow of corn marigolds

Orange and blue from Californian poppies
and cornflowers in the author's garden

Crocosmia 'Lucifer' is a winning
combination of red and green

Harmony and contrast

Knowledge of the colour wheel can be particularly valuable
to gardeners as a guide for how to put plants together. It is
obvious and instinctive that flowers whose colours sit next to
each other in the wheel will be harmonious when grouped in
a border. Soft washes of purple, mauve, pink and white are
going to be soothing to look at, so you can hardly go wrong
by planting together the blue of catmint, the pink of musk
mallow, white of cosmos and purple of lavender. It is safe and
comforting, calming and reassuring.

But familiarity with the colour wheel means that you
can play around with dynamic opposites, the ones that lie
across the wheel from each other and which are known as
complementary colours. They are simultaneously vivacious
and balanced when placed together. Orange and blue, red and
green, purple and yellow seem to increase in intensity due
to what is known as simultaneous contrast; a colour seems
to change depending on the background against which it is
placed. The scrambling flame flower of Chile, *Tropaeolum
speciosum*, a vivid red type of nasturtium, truly sings out when
grown against the deep green of a yew hedge. *Crocosmia*
'Lucifer' is such a striking plant because of its combination of
brilliant red-orange flowers and lushly green leaves.

The late Rosemary Verey used the complementary colours of yellow and purple in her famous laburnum tunnel at Barnsley House in Gloucestershire. Here, tall alliums reach up to almost touch the hanging tresses of laburnum flowers in a much-imitated combination. Very popular as a lecturer in the United States, this grande-dame of gardening had a wonderful eye for colour and she was much in demand as a garden designer. Other complementary colours are equally lively. Blue and orange are truly zingy when put together, as in the pairing of cornflowers and Californian poppies. The same permutation in spring comes from orange tulips emerging from a sea of blue forget-me-nots.

The famous laburnum tunnel at Barnsley House, England

The design for one of the five small gardens at Herterton House in Northumberland, England, was inspired by the work of twentieth century colourist painters, Klee and Mondrian. Here the compositions of Mondrian, his division of space by black lines into varying sizes of squares and rectangles, has influenced the strong design that underpins this surprising and exciting garden. Instead of flower borders that are viewed from one side, the right-angled paths lead in and through the colour-themed planting creating a sensual experience.

There is a subtle layer of meaning to the colours in this garden for they represent the passage of time throughout the day. This symbolism ebbs out from the walls of the seventeenth century house, the colours flowing out across the garden space. Nearest the house are the delicate yellows, pinks, creams and whites of dawn. The blocks of colour gather in intensity until the beds are vibrant with orange and blue, reminiscent of the sun at its zenith in a cloudless sky. Lastly, come the violent colours of sunset: reds, blacks and deep purples, with cooler blues and silvers to either side. It is as if a painting had been laid out upon the ground, translated into three dimensions but constantly evolving with the seasons.

This idea of seeing a border not from one side but by participating in it often underpins prairie planting and the style of the New Perennial plant movement. Seen from a number of viewpoints, it tends to use large blocks and drifts of a single colour. It often looks as if a painter has laden a thick brush with watercolours before daubing the paint in great undulating sweeps of purple, pink and red or yellow, orange and apricot. As autumn progresses and the flowers give way to much-valued seed heads, there is a beauty in the calm browns, ochre, copper and beige of grasses and perennials.

Swathes of colour in Piet Oudolf's planting at Pensthorpe Millennium Garden, England

Mondrian-inspired flower garden at Herterton House, England

Palest colours at Sissinghurst Castle in Kent, England

Using a single colour

That influential gardener, Gertrude Jekyll, enjoyed designing single colour gardens in which one colour predominates, but she declared that it was not worth spoiling a project for the sake of a word. If a blue garden is crying out for the injection of a cleverly placed complementary colour, then it is not worth adhering too strictly to the theme. A limited palette can work equally well in a contemporary setting as in a Jekyll-inspired romantic garden. The restricted colour scheme can be ideal for small, city spaces, or provide unity over a large area. The quality that a particular colour has affects the emotions. Hot colours - orange, red and yellow – are lively, exciting and dynamic. Cool colours – violet, soft blue, green – are tranquil and muted. They are calming and can make the garden seem larger than it is. As the eye sees it, cool colours retreat, hot colours advance.

Then there is white. Vita Sackville-West at Sissinghurst Castle in Kent set the fashion for numerous white gardens with her use of the palest of colours: silver, white, green and grey. It was designed to be seen in the evening when whites really come into their own, shining out in the dusk or glowing by moonlight. Yellow can have the same effect as in evening primrose, whose nightly opening flowers can appear luminous by twilight. This is illustrated by the memory of an English family who could see their way to the air-raid shelter at the bottom of their garden thanks to the lines of evening primrose on either side of the path.

The opposite of the single colour theme is the anarchy of the cottage garden. Here anything goes and that is its charm. Surprising effects come about from self-sown plants and from throwing the whole rainbow together. There may be bits that jar but the eye quickly moves on, seeking pleasing combinations. This haphazard mix can be joyful in its freedom, in its lacking of conventions, in its sheer randomness. It is as if paint has been thrown at the canvas, resulting in unexpected pairings of colours.

Strong colours are particularly suited to hot climates. In the work of landscape architect Steve Martino in the Southwest of the USA colour plays a hugely important part. His aesthetic often draws on the desert ecology around the house, with walls painted in colours borrowed from the desert plants. In this sharp light, shadows play against the yellows, reds, oranges and deep blues of the blocks of walls, bringing a consciousness of the passage of time throughout the day. His keen eye for colour makes his gardens bold and dramatic and entirely suited to their landscape.

Strong forms and colours in this Steve Martino garden, Phoenix, Arizona, USA

ABOVE
Japanese chequerboard moss garden

RIGHT
**A green rope of topiary at Bourton
House Garden, England**

'Green is also a colour'

Gertrude Jekyll once famously said that 'green is also a colour'. Green provides the background against which so many other colours are seen, which is why it needs a section all of its own. Hugely variable, it spans a gamut of hues from the palest lemon-green of spring through rich leaf-green to the near black-green of dark conifer woods. Many of the names that we use to describe this versatile colour are derived from plants: apple, olive, fern, lime, pistachio, asparagus, mint and pine.

A soothing colour, green is believed to slow down the heart rate and lower blood pressure. It is said to promote balance and calm, to relieve stress, to relax the muscles and slow the breathing rate. It connects us with the natural world more than any other colour, and its effects on mood have made it the preferred choice for hospital walls. There is a meditative quality to green that has made it an important element in Japanese temple gardens. The serene beauty of the moss garden reached its apotheosis in the Saiho-ji temple in Kyoto, a Rinzai Zen Buddhist temple with over 120 species of moss spreading their calming greenery around the Golden Pond at its centre. Designed for meditation, this is known as a stroll garden, the shape of the pond representing the Japanese character for 'heart' or 'spirit'.

Cloud pruned topiary in a Spanish villa garden designed by Fernando Caruncho

The Japanese style of training trees into forms resembling clouds is known as 'cloud pruning' or Nawaki, which translates as 'garden tree'. This highly stylised practice involves clipping trees and shrubs to create a perfect aesthetic of the plants' essence. The trunk and branches support rounded, sculpted shapes, which look particularly striking after a fall of snow. It has now become popular worldwide with gardeners experimenting with a wide range of species. Like topiary, cloud pruned trees bring a real presence to the winter garden when many other plants have gone into dormancy, as well as giving a feeling of age and permanency.

Topiary is a European style of pruning that dates back to Roman gardens. Pliny the Younger describes all manner of artificial shapes adorning the garden of his Tuscan villa: obelisks, animals, figures, ships and inscriptions in clipped box. Excavations at Fishbourne Palace near Chichester in England have revealed the layout of formal hedging, an elaborate pattern which has been recreated using box and which gives a feel of the original Roman garden.

Quirky shapes have evolved over years at Levens Hall, Cumbria, England

There is something very solid and reassuring about topiary gardens, partly due to the presence of so much green. It is a colour that does not cause eye fatigue and its restful qualities make it a superb background to colourful flowers. At Levens Hall in England's Cumbria, the magnificent and crazy topiary shapes that date back to 1694 make a quirky backdrop for formal gardens of brightly coloured bedding plants. The topiary has changed over time, evolving into the much loved, mainly abstract shapes that tower over the garden of this historic house. It is sculpture in greenery, eccentric and full of fun.

Green flowers are also fun. Being unexpected they have an oddity, an appealing eccentricity. Take for example the green rose plantain, *Plantago major* 'Rosularis', a strange form that delighted medieval gardeners who were often on the lookout for unusual plants. What appear to be rounded rose-like green flowers are really a mass of bracts, modified leaves with the appearance of petals. Being reliant on their bracts rather than actual flowers, they last for far longer in the garden. A whole border can be made around curious green flowers, using euphorbias, Bells of Ireland, *Zinnia* 'Envy', hellebores, *Rudbeckia* 'Green Wizard', *Gladiolus* 'Green Star', green chrysanthemums, ladies mantle and *Nicotiana alata* 'Lime Green'. For spring there are the dainty blooms of *Hacquetia epipactus,* grown with green primroses and the white and green tulip 'Spring Green'.

ABOVE
Houseleeks form a green roof on this shed in New Zealand

RIGHT
Patrick Blanc designed this green wall on Musee de Quay Branly, Paris

Green no longer needs to be confined to the garden but can envelope the house, its roof and walls. It is a way of counteracting the loss of habitat from building, the clothing of plants being soothing to the eye. Although the idea dates right back to the Hanging Gardens of Babylon, it has recently taken off thanks to modern technology. The French botanist Patrick Blanc has been innovative in his use of hydroponic systems to provide the water and nutrients needed to maintain vertical walls of planting which not only transform the appearance of urban buildings but also keep them cool. For the passer-by the effect on mood of a wall of green is calming and stress relieving. Similarly, roofs of turf or other greenery have restorative qualities.

Turf in its various forms is a large element of many gardens but there has been a recent interest in landforms. These sculptures of earth, greened by turf, are a modern interpretation of the mount of medieval gardens or the changed landscapes of the eighteenth century. Very often playful, offering elevated views, incorporating raised turf labyrinths or creating new physical forms from the land itself, they invite fresh ways of seeing. Contemporary design blends with the past in Kim Wilkie's response to the eighteenth century mount at Boughton Park in Northamptonshire, England. The obverse of the mount becomes an inverted pyramid sunk seven metres into the land. The greenery of the landform makes a frame for the sheet of water within that reflects the sky.

The restful effect of the colour green is what makes the jungle garden such a favourite for small city spaces. Here within high, sheltered walls a personal oasis can be created, where the colour green in its many forms shuts out the busy world. Palms, banana trees, ferns, phormiums and bamboos can be used to create a tropical paradise where foliage is far more important than flowers.

Whether you choose to use a single colour or a profusion of colours in your garden design, colour is what makes the garden come truly alive.

Kim Wilkie's landform 'Orpheus' at Boughton Park, England

PRINCIPLE 6
FORM AND TEXTURE

PRINCIPLE 6
FORM AND TEXTURE

Colour comes and goes throughout
the growing season, dependent on
the transient glory of flowers. Form
and texture can ebb and flow too as
leaves unfurl, perennials stretch up
to the sun and the gardener prunes
and cuts. Evergreens retain their form
even in winter, the texture of their
foliage providing a background for
more fleeting events. Some pared
back gardens rely more on form and
texture than on flowers.

LEFT
A myriad of textures in these
eucalyptus seed heads and leaves

PREVIOUS PAGE
Ammi majus, feather grass and
golden oats at Perch Hill,
East Sussex, England

Softness of grasses and roughness of wood provide contrasting textures on this garden wall

Buxus balls and birch stems

Combining plant forms

Gardeners often talk about plant forms and in this context it means their volume and shape, their structure and distinctive character. The habit of a tree or shrub may be weeping, upright, columnar, twisted, flat-topped, cascading, arching or spreading; it is this multiplicity of plant shapes that give us so much to play with in making a garden. By positioning them in a dynamic way next to each other, they bring out each other's qualities.

Using just two plant forms, as in this example from Holland, pictured left, can make an exciting juxtaposition. The clipped box balls of varying sizes express a cushioned solidity in contrast to the rising stems of three birch trees, all artfully placed so that they make a scene of overlapping shapes. The rounded masses and vertical stems are then further enhanced by the assorted textures: the papery birch bark lined with fissures, the two different leaf sizes on the box.

Then there are the forms of herbaceous plants, their flowering heads shaped like spikes, umbrellas or domes, their huge variety of structures of stem and leaf. There are the strong verticals of iris and crocosmia leaves, the enormous head height spans of gunnera, the spires of delphinium and foxglove, the branching architecture of onopordum thistles. Each grouping of plants within a border is a picture in miniature; when deciding where to plant you can juggle the plants about, relying on instinct, noticing what shape looks best next to the other. Contrasting shape and foliage makes dynamic, vivid pictures, while similar forms bring calm and serenity.

Glistening bark on *Prunus serrula* 'Tibetan Cherry'

Texture

Texture is the surface quality of plants, the factor that influences the interplay of light and shadow falling on leaves. It is visual and tactile; it's impossible not to be drawn to run our fingers over the furry surface of *Stachys byzantina* 'lamb's ears' or the cool tresses of fennel. Sensory gardens, often planted in school and public areas, make the most of this tactile side of plants.

Texture is not only in leaves but also on bark, seed heads, roots or stems, and these give us an enormous range of textures. The mahogany polished bark of Tibetan cherry, the spreading mats of woolly thyme, the glossy leaves of a bay tree or the peeling bark of the birch all enhance our experience of the natural world.

It is even on flowers such as the wonderful hairy blooms of red or blue salvias. The flowers of sea hollies have rigid, rough heads with surrounding rays of spines, a lively contrast to softer perennial plants. The seed heads that are left in the winter garden give texture at a time of the year when we need visual stimuli, when the surface of the bark of trees also comes to the fore.

TOP LEFT
Prickly sea holly contrast with spires of purple salvia

ABOVE
Peeling bark on a silver birch

A whole range of textures play
against each other in this
grass border

The interplay of surfaces

To design your garden in an artful way you need to be open,
aware and observant, seeing one surface against another and
playing with shapes. Placing one leaf against another can be
a way of experimenting so that interesting juxtapositions can
be made between different textures. Exciting dynamics can
be created by going on instinct and really looking. Texture
is particularly associated with leaves. They may be fine,
rough, ferny and delicate, hairy, puckered or spiny. Each will
reflect the light and create shadows in differing ways, each
contributing to the feel and look of the garden.

ABOVE
Feathery fennel and rich dark iris flowers

LEFT
Silver cardoon leaves make a perfect
background to this delphinium spire

TOP LEFT
Delicate buttercups thread through
puckered hosta leaves

Setting plants of different forms and textures next to each other creates a varied tapestry. The light and airy look of grasses and prairie plants is given weight and contrast when punctuated by the bold leaves of acanthus or the silver architecture of cardoons. The delicate tracery plants, such as the ever-popular *Verbena bonariensis*, ferny-foliaged asparagus or the annual *Ammi majus*, are perfect counterpoints for dramatic large-leaf perennials. We can create contrast with fine against coarse, bold against delicate, spiky against lacy, all adding to the feel and atmosphere of the garden.

It's these exciting combinations that create mini pictures within a border. Variety excites the eye. Bold hosta leaves make a corrugated background for finely stalked buttercups, the fresh green tracery of fennel a contrast to the striking leaves of irises and the fine texture of grasses complements the purple cone heads of Echinacea in prairie planting. It's these textural contrasts that bring dynamism to the garden, views that alter with distance. Close up we can appreciate the effect of one type of surface against another. Our view changes as we stand further back and we see the mass effect of leaves.

A small tree that has outstanding form is the contorted hazel, *Corylus avellana* 'Contorta'. Its crazy branches are best seen in winter when there is no leaf cover, especially when snow highlights its extraordinary twists and turns. Its catkins and young leaves also look attractive but once the leaves mature they have a coarse texture, shrouding the branches with puckered foliage. This is a case of good form, poor texture, so this wonderful and mad tree is best planted where tall perennials can flower in front of it in summer.

The choice of materials also gives a range of textures, but apply too many and the garden becomes piecemeal and cluttered. As with plants, observation of the way that light falls, the way that it creates shadows and depths, can influence how they are placed. Add the varying surfaces of plants as well and one texture can be played off against the other. This may sound complex but looking is key. Keep an open mind, try things out and enjoy the process of experimenting with form and texture.

The crazy branches of the contorted hazel, *Corylus avellana* 'Contorta'

PRINCIPLE 7
RHYTHM

PRINCIPLE 7
RHYTHM

Rhythm is created by the repetition of lines and shapes. Just as in the brushstrokes of a painting, this repetition of visual elements gives vitality and movement to what we see. It helps to move our eyes around the garden, drawing attention to the foreground, then to the background, whilst taking in the various colours and shapes and constantly shifting our focus. It aids the visual flow, bringing unity to the whole, but most of all it creates dynamic movement.

LEFT
Spiky rhythm in the leaves of an aloe in South Africa

PREVIOUS PAGE
Different sized pebbles form a rhythmic mosaic shaped like peacock feathers

Conifers draw the eye upwards in this Welsh garden

There is rhythm in the detail, more vibrant in some plants than in others, as well as in the whole picture that the garden creates and the way that its various elements are put together. We can choose plants that form exciting rhythmic shapes, from the undulating lines of the humble leek in the vegetable garden to the exotic, impressed shapes left by the unfolding leaves of agaves. Agaves and aloes, with their regular rows of red-tipped spikes, are good examples of repeated shapes within a plant that create an almost musical rhythm.

Repetition

Rhythm can be flowing or interrupted, managed or freeform, staccato or smooth. We can create it by repeating the shapes of plants, stems or trunks of trees. The artful placement of repeated shapes leads the eye to a focal point or enables it to move restlessly around the garden, changing as we walk through the space. The trunks in a tree-lined avenue, the snaking course of a path, the curving outline of a border or neat lines of produce in the vegetable garden are all examples of rhythm from repetition. Just as in music, the spacing is important; this may be the intervals between the upright forms of trees, the gaps between topiary domes or the distance between flower filled containers.

ABOVE
Japanese stroll garden

TOP LEFT
Rhythmic patterns are formed by this line of trees in winter

Repeated colours add cohesion to this border

Repeated colours and shapes in a border bring unity and cohesion. A traditional herbaceous border, crowded with cottage varieties in summer, often needs key plants to reappear at intervals throughout its length to give structure. This might be the strong magenta of *Geranium psilostemum* cropping up at regular times to draw the whole thing together, or the repeated froth of lime-green ladies mantle alternating with the purple-blue of catmint along the front edge. A border can be planned around a few signature plants, a pattern that brings it together.

Modern planting that relies on simplicity and harmony often uses rhythmic repetitions. James Alexander-Sinclair designed a contemporary garden next to the visitor centre on the Scottish Isle of Bute, a design inspired by an unfurled paperclip. Wide parallel lines of repeated grasses and perennials echo the horizontal lines of weathered hardwood that clothe this innovative building. It's a bit paradoxical but the kind of grasses and plants that contribute to free flowing prairie planting often make suitable species for managed, repetitive designs.

LEFT
Jaques Wirtz designed these rhythmic parallel hedges at Cloostermans, Belgium

ABOVE
Repetitious grass planting in contemporary design by James Alexander-Sinclair on the Isle of Bute, Scotland

Snaking line of grasses

Creating movement

Those prairie plants are particularly good at showing the passage of wind through the garden; grasses ripple, their stems curving, their heads bobbing. Perennials such as loosestrife, verbena, scabious, meadowsweet and golden rod bend with the wind contributing to the experience of movement. The garden becomes a kinetic sculpture, its overlapping layers constantly on the move, activated by the currents of air. It becomes a quite different experience on a breezy day to the mood created on a calm, still day. These kind of wind-catching plants bring the weather to our notice; seen through a window we can gauge what it is doing outside from the shifting, restless grasses. They make visible what is normally invisible.

Using water and stones

Water brings with it a new rhythm, both visual and audible. Just as the right plants can be used to catch the wind, the artful positioning of rocks, ledges or pebbles can interrupt the flow of water creating dynamic patterns. Using natural or manmade materials, water can be made to create different rhythms: sleek flowing shapes for a calm mood or interrupted, unpredictable and invigorating patterns. The sound of water brings another dimension to the garden, an audible confirmation of its visual appearance. The deep tone of water dropping from a height into a fern-lined pool, the soft murmur as it runs over cobbles or the staccato rhythm as it bounds over randomly placed rocks fill the garden with different moods.

LEFT
Water flowing through stones creates different sounds

RIGHT
Waterfall in ferns

The shadows of this low willow fence add another dimension

The movement of water can be imitated in stones. Narrow but round-shouldered slates or thin, upright pebbles create the best rhythms. When closely laid together, they appear more fluid than plump cobbles. These repeated but irregular shapes can lead the eye a dance, swirling around larger rocks in imitation of water. The shadows of stones and other materials create further rhythms. River-washed cobbles make an attractive surface that creates wavy shadows thanks to their rounded shapes. Regularly spaced trees lay echoes of themselves across a path or lawn. A fence casts a version of itself seen only when the sun shines. Shadows are often not taken into account when designing a garden but they allow us to experience something new and fleeting.

Hedges

Fluid movement can also be imitated in the line of a hedge. So often used as the boundary of a geometric shape, hedges can be liberated from these constraints to create wonderful free flowing forms. Used in a contemporary way, they can

Shaped hedge rising out of soft planting at Le Jardin Plume, France

undulate and snake across a garden space, create rippling forms or echo the far landscape. At Le Jardin Plume near Rouen in France, Patrick and Sylvie Quibel have sculpted hedges into wave-like shapes that bring to mind the fins of a dolpin or the spines of an agave. Hedges slice through the ebullient perennials and grasses, carving out sweeping curves and bringing a solidity to the freedom of the planting. It is a perfect synthesis of prairie planting with an underlying formal structure from French gardens of the past, a mixture of geometry and anarchy.

The repetitive lines of different materials also create rhythm in the garden. The horizontal banding of willow hurdles or the upright stakes of a picket fence with spikes of lavender peeping through, both lead our eyes through different planes. Too much repetition, however, can be too harmonious and the result less exciting. Too much and there is visual overload, so there needs to be the right balance. Using a combination of natural and designed rhythms creates flow across the picture of the garden just as it does across a painter's canvas.

PRINCIPLE 8
PLANTS

PRINCIPLE 8
PLANTS

Of course no garden would be a garden without plants, and although I have mentioned various names throughout the previous principles, this chapter is not meant to be a specific guide to the many plants available. There are many wonderful resources available that will tell you all you need to know about individual plants and trees. What follows is a guide to thinking about plants in a more general way in relation to garden design.

LEFT
Successive heights in a cottage border

PREVIOUS PAGE
Colourful suburban garden

Creating layers

If you think about how an artist might build up an oil painting, opaque layer upon successive layer, or a watercolour with its veils of semi-transparency, this is how artful garden design may also be approached. The garden may have solid objects, shrubs, topiary or blocks of planting, or it may have semi-transparent filmy grasses, thin stalks and lacy flowers that still allow us to glimpse fragments of the further distance. The other opportunity for creating layers is to plant in tiers from ground level right up to trees.

The traditional border is built up in stages, with low growing plants along the front edge, rising in height to the most majestic plants at the back. Beautiful but labour-intensive, this border relies particularly on perennial plants that are laid out in large drifts so that no bare soil is visible in summer. Island beds follow the same kind of format with tall plants at their centre, descending in height to every edge so that they can be viewed from all sides. By arranging the plants in stepped-up layers the border becomes a glorious mass of colours and forms, dropping down in generous sweeps and arcs to the front edge.

A contemporary twist to this traditional design is to bring some of those tall growing plants towards the front and in particular to use perennials and grasses that give a semi-transparent effect. The flower border is seen through veils of planting, the colour washes similar to watercolours; the colour beyond is stronger where it is seen directly and softened where grass heads blur across it. Some plants have become favourites for this type of planting. The classic one is *Verbena bonariensis*, its wiry stems topped with little clusters of vivid purple flowers that attract butterflies. It has an open quality so that you can see through it to the plants behind; its flowers appear to float in the air.

The burnet family, *Sanguisorba*, has gained in popularity recently for the same reason. Its thin stems hold aloft bottlebrush flowers in colours ranging from white through sugar pink to burgundy. Other plants include the delicate, arching blooms of angel's fishing rods, the lacy green foliage of fennel and meadow rue, spiky Russian sage and, of course, grasses. One of the best, as it name suggests, is *Molinia* 'Transparent', which creates a gauzy screen, its delicate seed heads bobbing and dancing in the wind. It is rather like seeing through a lace curtain, the combination of the foreground and background plants constantly changing as you walk past. The same look can be achieved in winter when the stalks and seed heads of perennials become thinned and rimed with frost.

These raised beds in California create a garden on many different levels

These layers add depth in the same way as layers of paint, building up the garden picture bit by bit until it is satisfying and stimulating to the eye. This gives a sense of complexity, of not quite knowing how far back the boundary lies, of mystery and of expansiveness. Planting in this way can make a garden appear larger than it is. As well as creating a feeling of depth, another way of layering is in making tiered heights. This increases the interest in a different way. A series of raised beds can elevate the design from a flat space, their level planes counterpoised by the upright shapes of plants. To this can be added climbers on poles or obelisks, the fastigiated forms of conifers, anything that lifts the eye up after it has travelled across the horizontal plane.

Using different levels

If we look out from a window at a succession of ascending terraces, the flower filled levels rise up vertically creating a far more interesting effect than that of a flat plane. Stepped the other way, terracing leads the eye up to the house, a technique much employed by the great Arts and Crafts landscape architect Thomas Mawson. He restructured the land, moving great quantities of earth, for the grounds of large houses in the English Lake District, setting off and elevating them so that they sat well in the landscape. The gardens of this period also often included sunken areas of lawn or pond enclosed by raised stone walls, with curved steps descending into them, spangled with little daisies or ferns growing in the gaps. Sitting within these sunken gardens you feel enveloped by the layers of plants and walls that rise up around you, a place to dream away an afternoon.

Hedges can fulfil the same function when planted on different levels or clipped to different heights. Starting with low box hedging they can be worked up through stages, the middle stage made from yew or beech, up to the elevated mass of pleached hornbeam, its 'hedge' raised up on the stilts of bare, grey trunks. What is created is a series of parallel blocks in varying shades of green and alternating textures of leaves. Pleached trees are also very useful in screening an unwanted view, either with the greenery of hornbeam or with the pink blossom and colourful fruit of crab apples, whilst still allowing views beneath the canopy.

Terraces at Hestercombe, England, create a multi-layered effect

From ground level up through successive heights to trees, a multi-layered garden is not only inspiring but also of great benefit to wildlife. Birds feel safe when given the corridors of branches to slip along unseen, the protection of shrubs in which to nest and perch, fruits to eat and the seed heads of perennials to feast on. Low lying foliage provides homes for frogs, toads and newts, stone walls a sanctuary for lizards and small mammals, flowers nectar for insects and ponds places to drink and bathe. A variety of heights means a variety of habitats with places to eat, breed and shelter.

ABOVE
These pleached trees could block an unwelcome view whilst allowing glimpses through their trunks

LEFT
Pleached lime avenue in winter

Every layer of planting in this forest garden is productive

Forest Gardening

Forest gardening is an organic, sustainable method of producing a range of plants for food. Based on the ecosystem of a woodland, and therefore excellent for attracting wildlife, it is designed as a series of layers similar to a forest habitat. Pioneered by Robert Hart on the Welsh borders, it is inspired by ancient techniques of cultivation, including that of the Aztecs. Hart developed his forest garden in an old orchard using the existing trees as a starting point for seven 'storeys', successive layers he termed: canopy, low-tree, shrub, herbaceous, ground cover, 'rhizosphere' (root zone) and vertical. Here he grew fruit, 'top' fruit on the old trees added to by currant bushes and berries, nut trees such as hazel, vegetables, herbs and low growing edible plants. The 'rhizosphere' included those plants harvested for their roots or tubers and extra height came from climbers and vines.

His view was that this system worked better than the traditional rows of monoculture vegetables with quite separate fruit areas; that by imitating the layers in a woodland habitat, there would be less effort and fewer pests and diseases. He believed it could be the harmonious blueprint for gardening worldwide in small spaces such as in cities and therefore of great benefit. His own plot was about the size of a large town garden, inspiration he hoped for a mass of small city forests that could result in 'maximum output for minimum labour'. It's a three dimensional, no dig system imitating the many layers in a natural forest.

Change and the seasons

The ebb and flow of growth according to the seasons is the most challenging aspect of creating an artful garden. The creative process has to cope with the passage of time, not just the appearance of a single day. How familiar is the cry of gardeners that 'you should have seen it last week.' Yet it is this fragility and impermanence that makes gardening so very beautiful, the sense that nothing stays the same and must be valued for the moment in which it exists. In this way the garden can be seen as a metaphor for life.

Gardening connects us with the rhythm of the year, making us aware of even the smallest changes. There is really no start to 'the season' for it is a continuous cycle. For the professional gardener the work done in late autumn is crucial as it sets the scene for spring. Preparation of borders, dividing and moving plants into new positions, planting bulbs and re-evaluating the design are all part of the planning process necessary before the winter. In this way imagination is needed to see what it will look like months ahead. As the seasons progress they are marked by annual events, each a reminder of previous seasons in a cyclical motion, looked forward to, enjoyed and then passing. This rhythm plays out like a piece of music with crescendos at certain times of the year.

Colours abound in this mixed autumn raised bed

ABOVE
Cherry blossom festivals in Japan
are a celebration of spring

RIGHT
Snowdrops, heralds of spring

Spring

In Japan the blooming of the cherry blossom has been celebrated for centuries by picnicking under the flower laden trees. Known as Hanami, these cherry blossom-viewing parties attract huge crowds with the best spots reserved early. As spring moves from the southern islands towards the north it takes some three to four months and part of the national weather report is dedicated to its progress. The shortness of the flowering time of the cherry is richly symbolic of the ephemeral nature of life, with the flower clusters being likened to clouds. Sometimes lit up at night, the most sought after views of cherry trees are often in combination with temples, castles, water or mountains.

Cherry blossom festivals happen in cities all over the world, often where Japanese have settled or given trees as gestures of friendship to other countries. Vancouver, Washington DC, San Francisco, Copenhagen, Berlin and many other cities celebrate, with viewing parties and Japanese arts, the short lifespan of this delicate spring flower. There are other flowers that, when they reach a peak, are also celebrated for their seasonal beauty. When grown in huge drifts, the snowdrop, symbol of regeneration and the fresh year, draws large numbers of visitors to estates and parks. Scotland has an annual Snowdrop Festival that takes place at over 50 gardens. As with Hanami, flowering times vary according to the weather so people eagerly await the best time to see these serene white flowers en masse, sometimes lit up at night or with the inimitable background of a Scottish castle.

Other high points in the floral year are celebrated in festivals that are centred on chrysanthemums, roses, lilacs, apple blossom and the phenomenal colour of the flowering of the bulb fields in the Netherlands. Tourists travel from all over the world to see the incredible spectacle of massed blooms, to revel in the blocks and lines of colour akin to abstract paintings. There are many millions of blooms in endless stripes of yellow, red, orange, purple and gold added to by the scent of hyacinths.

Intense colour in Keukenhof Gardens, the Netherlands

RIGHT
Bedding schemes in public parks are designed for maximum colour

ABOVE
Great Dixter in spring

Designing for all seasons

However, spring is not the only season for fabulous plantings. Exuberant colour dominates in the traditional bedding schemes of public parks. The changing year is clearly delineated in the successional planting that takes place twice, sometimes three times a year. Massed bulbs and primulas, wallflowers and pom-pom daisies herald spring, followed by hardy annuals for early summer, then late season vibrant colour from cannas, bananas and other tender, sub-tropical plants. It's high maintenance and expensive but betokens the passing seasons in a unique way. The scent of wallflowers in a public park in spring creates lasting memories.

Designs for bedding schemes are worked out on graph paper or using computer programmes but the mixed border is far more complex to design for change. In some large gardens, borders can be dedicated to a single season, as at Floors Castle in the Scottish Borders. Here, three extensive borders are designed to be seen in early summer, full summer and autumn. By dedicating each to a specific time of year they provide fulsome, eye dazzling colour at that particular moment.

For the mixed border of perennials, climbers, annuals, grasses, shrubs and bulbs it takes experience and an openness to experimentation to create constantly changing, constantly exciting visual pictures. This has been sublimely achieved at Great Dixter in England's East Sussex. The late Christopher Lloyd was an expert at mixing colours, at creating a constantly evolving tapestry and was always fresh with new ideas. As the Great Dixter website says 'He spent his lifetime practising and refining his art', for art it is when gardening at this level. His head gardener and friend, Fergus Garrett, carries on this work, constantly looking for new plant combinations in the mixed borders. He is unafraid to put colours together that others might fear would clash.

The famous Long Border at Great Dixter is a carefully woven picture of structural plants and climbers, underplanted with bulbs, washed with the brushstrokes of perennials, spiced with self-seeders and vibrant with brightly coloured annuals. There is no bare soil to be seen. Plants are combined in dazzling ways, using colour, shape, texture, repetition and balance. Clusters of pots are arranged in changeable patterns, varying heights, contrasting foliage and shapes, each combination creating a new picture. The Exotic Garden is a revelation for England; tender plants create a sumptuous, sensuous late season garden of orange, red, purple and yellow with lush foliage in a courtyard full of butterflies. From the delicate orchard colours of spring, the brilliance of tulips and annual bedding plants and the diverse summer displays to the Exotic Garden in autumn, Great Dixter is a place to truly experience the changing seasons all in one great garden.

TOP
Great Dixter in winter

TOP LEFT
Christopher Lloyd designed the Exotic Garden at Great Dixter in East Sussex, England

PRINCIPLE 9
MATERIALS

PRINCIPLE 9
MATERIALS

The foundation of a garden is its hard landscaping, the layout that supports the layers of planting. It is the most sculptural element, strong in its physicality, underlying everything. The design can be thought of purely in terms of a pattern. This is particularly obvious at garden shows with their exemplary exhibition gardens, where you can often clearly see the squares, circles, rectangles and the basic geometry. It is there in the clean lines of stone, wood and metal. It is just as important in creating atmosphere as the plants that will later embellish it.

LEFT
A range of materials are used in this Chelsea Flower Show display garden

PREVIOUS PAGE
Slate and pebbles form this colourful spiral

Slates are laid on edge in this recycled garden

Simplicity of materials often makes for a more effective design. Limiting the different types of surface to three in any particular space brings a unity to that design and prevents it from being cluttered. A large garden can be given harmony if a narrow range of textures is used. As with any rule this can be turned on its head and a deliberate use of a large mass of contrasting materials can make an effective statement providing they are laid out in some coherent whole. This could be a plethora of recycled objects, chosen for their randomness but assembled to create something well structured and complete in itself.

Creating a sense of place

A sense of place is also important so that the materials have an authenticity that is appropriate to the site. Vernacular buildings gain much of their charm from their relevance to a particular landscape. There is an integrity as well as sustainability if stone, slate, brick or wood comes from the surrounding land. A brick path will echo the walls of a brick building, stone walls have resonance with a stone built house and the right gravel can pick up on the colours of a house exterior. Using a local style can give a garden an immediate sense of being a part of its landscape and tradition.

There is a strong sense of place at the Cerulean Tower Hotel rock garden, Tokyo

TOP
Old bricks bring a warmth to this garden path

BOTTOM
Brick and stone create a swirling mosaic surface

Brick and stone

Sensitivity to the quality of each material is central to the artful approach to garden design. If brick is to be used, there are many sizes, colours and textures of brick, depending on the local clay and the land from which it is made. Machine-made bricks have a uniformity, a regularity that can be suitable for some garden designs. Alternatively, handmade bricks have a range of colours due to irregular firing as well as uneven edges. Sourced from architectural salvage they have a uniqueness and subtlety that is sympathetic to the planting.

It is the same with stone and its vast range of colours and textures. Where a house is built from locally quarried stone, it is fitting to use the same kind of stone in gravel form for the paths. Laying down granite chips, bought in from another part of the country, when a house is built from limestone is wasteful in terms of energy, unsympathetic to the building and lacking in local distinctiveness. In an area where field boundaries are made from dry stone walls, a garden wall made the same way has an authenticity about it. Add cement mortar and it looks wrong for its location, though lime mortar may be fitting, as well as being better for plants. In the English Lake District, the sense of individuality of the area is strongly present in the harmonious use of slate quarried from the nearby fells. Slate combines well with brick and wood in garden surfaces and was used to great effect by the landscape architect Sir Edwin Lutyens who often laid slate in upward facing rhythmic patterns. Observation is often the starting point for any artwork so look around you to see what feels right from the surrounding land.

ABOVE
Brambles are grown against this wooden panel

RIGHT
Aged wood path in a Zen style moss garden, Millburn, New Jersey, USA

Wood

Wood too can be harvested from the local region, bringing integrity to the design. An aesthetic response to and appreciation of the qualities of different woods contributes to garden design. Willow edging and panels may be woven from locally sourced trees. Indigenous trees can be used for pergolas, garden buildings and structures. Wood may be planed, smooth, wavy, rough, silver with age or coloured by linseed oil, uneven, knotted, grainy or chiselled. Extremely versatile, it can be untreated, painted, lime-washed, stained or given history and texture by layers of peeling paint.

Manufactured and recycled materials

Artificial stone is often used in the manufacture of garden
statuary, benches, ornaments and balustrades. Compared to
concrete, its properties allow it to acquire a patina of lichen
and moss more quickly, giving it a feeling of age. Made from
crushed stone that is reconstituted and set in a mould, it
is blended with cement mortar to form a good imitation of
natural stone. This is not a new technique; it has a history
going right back to the twelfth century repair of the medieval
fortifications of Carcassonne in France.

In urban areas it may be more fitting to use manufactured
materials such as frosted glass, zinc, metal, coloured
perspex or fibreglass. Rusted metal provides a very suitable
background to plant forms; rusted metal poles and supports
have the ability to blend into a flower border. Metal gabions
fixed as retaining walls can be filled with bricks and tiles that
might otherwise have gone to landfill. In an effort to reduce
wastefulness, coupled with the search for inspiring new
materials, many garden designers are turning to new ideas
in recycled surfaces for garden paths and features. Whether
they are new or old, what is most important is that they are of
good quality.

ABOVE
**Metal squares reflect the sky in
this London garden**

LEFT
**Blue glass and green marbles are
used as an unusual mulch beneath
bamboos**

LEFT
**An eclectic mix of materials
in a bug hotel**

RIGHT
**Rainbow path made from rubber at
the Eden Project, Cornwall, England**

Rubber mulch made from recycled tyres comes in a variety of colours; rubber paths are used for a rainbow effect at the Eden Project in Cornwall, southwest England. Broken slate, the refuse from quarrying or from roofing, can be used to make paths or mulch borders. Crushed seashells are a waste product of the fishing industry. They make an unusual mulch with the added benefit that slugs and snails find it harder to traverse their jagged surfaces. Bug hotels are an eclectic mix of the manmade and the natural. They use a huge variety of items to make potential homes for insects: hollow angelica or bamboo stems, grilles, holed bricks, slate, stacked terracotta pots, straw and wood drilled with holes.

There is a wealth of possibility from reusing objects. Reclaimed materials make a garden look established and impart a sense of history. Reclamation yards are a great source of ideas, with interesting artefacts to include in the design. Working out how to incorporate recycled objects sometimes requires imagination. This has been done for many years in allotments or community gardens where sheds, bed edgings, greenhouses and all manner of garden features have been made from found materials. Greenhouses made from old telephone kiosk glass, sheds created from wood that has seen a previous life, decorative finials and roof crests as well as mismatched windows all lend an individual charm to the functional. There is an enormous amount of room for creativity and the results are quirky and personal.

Recycled garden with greenhouse of plastic bottles

PRINCIPLE 10
IDEAS AND
EFFECTS

PRINCIPLE 10
IDEAS AND EFFECTS

There are many ways to create an artful garden design so this final principle focuses on stimulating your imagination to consider how to make your garden reflect you. You may prefer a more formal style or you may like a quirkier approach. Then again, you might like the idea of creating a garden in a traffic island.

However natural a garden may appear it is always an artificial environment. Fashions come and go and throughout history the balance between formality and informality, between control and naturalism, has ebbed and flowed.

In early centuries, untamed nature felt threatening and gardeners sought to impose control over it. Throughout the Renaissance period there was a relaxation of this tight control and quasi-natural groves of trees could more safely be planted and delighted in. 'Wilderness' gardens of the seventeenth and eighteenth centuries in Europe and America were densely planted with trees and shrubs. These were designed wildernesses, with carefully planned rustic, meandering paths to lead and tease, often with surprises around the corner.

Laid out beyond the formal areas around the house, they were a way of creating a frisson of delight at 'wild' nature. They enticed with a hint of mystery, with a feeling of enclosure that led to small clearings or views down tree-lined avenues. The great landscape architect Lancelot 'Capability' Brown even lived in a house named Wilderness House within the walls of Hampton Court Palace where he worked as chief gardener in the late eighteenth century.

The nineteenth century saw a desire for domination over nature in the elaborate bedding schemes of the Victorians. This was then reacted against by William Robinson leading the way to more natural gardening and, later, the birth of the New Perennial movement. It is as if formality and informality stand at two opposite poles – complete imposition of will over nature versus the emulation of a wild landscape – and that all gardens are points along this scale. Often the resolution of this conflict is to have both, with the formal areas near the house, progressing towards the wilder areas further away. Or in the case of the Lutyens/Jekyll partnership, to have an underlying formal structure with free flowing planting softening its geometry.

The new naturalism

Experiments with emulating natural plant communities have grown out of the ecology movement and an interest in natural landscapes. Gardeners have looked at how plants grow together according to their locality and tried to copy these conditions. One of the most experimental is Keith Wiley who in 2004 began work on a four-acre site in Devon, England. He used mechanical diggers to sculpt the land into deep gullies, mounds, ridges and winding paths, creating a series of mini landscapes of different depths and heights, orientations and levels. The difference in height reaches 25-30ft in some places. The resulting microclimates allowed him to plant for many types of plant colonies: alpines, scree lovers, desert plants, meadows, bog and grassland. He calls it the 'new naturalism'.

Perennials and bulbs grow in interwoven drifts without reference to the colour wheel, which is as it occurs in nature. Keith takes particular inspiration from the landscapes of California, South Africa, the Mediterranean island of Crete and the scrubby woodland of the US/Canadian border. The plants don't necessarily have to come from these regions; the planting is more an expression of the essence of each place. If it feels right, he puts it in and if there was a rulebook he has thrown it out of the window.

Naturalistic planting in Keith Wiley's Wildside garden, Devon, England

Wild cow parsley froths through this split oak fence

Rocks, trees, and wild and cultivated plants combine at Villa Nordfjell, Sweden

Keith Wiley's way of transforming flat land into hills and canyons is a highly unusual approach to natural planting. Often gardeners have to go with what the land suggests, particularly in rocky areas. At the lakeside Villa Nordfjell in Sweden rocks break through the surface of the land and a peaceful wild garden has been made incorporating the lichen-covered rocks and native grasses. This is gentle gardening where it can be hard to distinguish between the landscape that is already there and the introduced planting.

Gardeners who seek inspiration from the wild only have to look at those haphazard events that have great natural beauty - such as the froth of cow parsley that erupts in the English countryside in May at the same time as hawthorn blossom, the sudden blooming of the desert in South Africa or the spangled, alpine meadows of Austria. These naturally occurring 'gardens' are made of many colours like the jumble of a cottage garden, yet they all blend together and nothing jars. It is very different to the careful colour scheme of the traditional herbaceous border and the use of a limited palette.

In allowing these types of plants their freedom, a kind of controlled chaos is reached, where there is delight in the anarchy of self-seeders, in the drifts of plants with spreading habits. Leaving seed heads to stand all winter gives protection to insects and wildlife, a structure for the crystals of frost to decorate and allows those opportunistic plants to seed themselves where they wish. Often it is these unplanned combinations of plants that bring unexpected pleasures.

Absolute control in rows of colourful cabbages, Villandry, France

Control over nature

At the other end of the scale is control. This rigid imposition of will over nature can be seen not only in the great historic formal gardens such as Villandry in France, but also in contemporary designs. Minimalist planting that concentrates on just a few key elements relies on the repetition of forms to create a strong, clean aesthetic. Grasses and cacti particularly lend themselves to this type of design due to their dynamic forms. Their shapes can trace regular patterns that exemplify control over nature and yet it is a kind of paradox as designers are often choosing native plants from a local habitat.

In the southwestern USA there are areas where the landscape is a dominant force. Here architects and garden designers have kept to simple forms using endemic plants to establish a dialogue between the wild and the cultivated. Landscape architect Steve Martino uses blocks of vivid colour on house walls and in outdoor rooms against which are seen the bold shapes of cacti, succulents and their shadows. Each view, either towards the dry landscape or within the garden spaces, is carefully positioned as a series of pictures. His designs celebrate the desert environment, revelling in the spectacular shapes of its flora, yet all is carefully controlled with regularly spaced cacti, views framed through openings and water emphasising the desert outside.

Bold cactus shapes in Steve Martino's dry desert garden

LEFT
**Regular planting of grasses,
Sonoma, USA**

RIGHT
Echlum in Napa Valley vineyard

The design of formal contemporary gardens usually relies on symmetry with strong axial lines, the geometry creating balance. For the planting, a few, choice species give a restrained effect; the emphasis is on plant shape rather than diversity. Geometric or flowing block planting of just one species of grass, artfully placed trees, clean lines of water features and modern sculpture create strong visuals. These two polar opposites form contemporary garden design: anarchy and control with all the grades and variations in between.

Topiary

There are other ways to exert control, but in a slightly more whimsical form. Because private gardens take time to evolve, the shrubs and hedges become misshapen over the years. The resulting lopsided or bulging shapes get clipped as they expand into quirky, moulded shapes like lumps of dough. An evergreen shrub may suggest the outline of a bird or animal and be clipped into shape, or what starts out life as a topiary peacock may become distorted over time into a fanciful imaginary bird. Birds are especially popular with topiarists as their forms lend themselves particularly well, with their sculpted figures roosting atop other clipped shapes.

Box and yew have long been the favoured materials for topiary forms, but there are other plants that are similarly malleable. Ivy grown around a frame can make a fast growing, faux topiary or be rigidly clipped against a wall to make fanciful shapes. It can be trained into swags against walls, crisscrossed to form latticework or shaped into hearts. Pyracantha, its lethal spines controlled by tight clipping, can be fan-trained against a wall, made to fit around windows and doors or formed into a series of parallel, horizontal lines. Designs like these can be planned and thought-out, but often they have resulted from the owner seeking to keep their wall shrubs under control and using imagination to make something entirely personal.

This is one of Chris Parsons' beautifully ephemeral dew art pieces

Creating ephemeral effects

Gardens never stay the same, though some go through more radical changes than others. It is this impermanence which prevents them from stultifying, and which, in their conception and maintenance, turns their finest examples into an art form. Some gardeners have taken this impermanence to its fullest extent, creating fleeting events on the background of the garden itself.

Perhaps the most transitory of all, the work of Englishman Chris Parsons is seen by very few people. He begins at dawn with a dew brushing technique that was evolved for bowling greens, golf courses and the tennis courts of Wimbledon to prevent fungal diseases. Using a wide brush, he sweeps patterns in the autumn dew on fine mornings, making contrasting stripes and swirls with the still gleaming dew-laden grass and the darker brushed areas. Vanishing within a few hours he records his work in photographs, a way of archiving this ephemeral moment similar to the temporary interventions of land art in the work of artists such as Richard Long and Andy Goldsworthy. Land art documents movement, change, fragility, decay and light and makes us re-evaluate the natural world. This evanescent art form can also be applied to gardens.

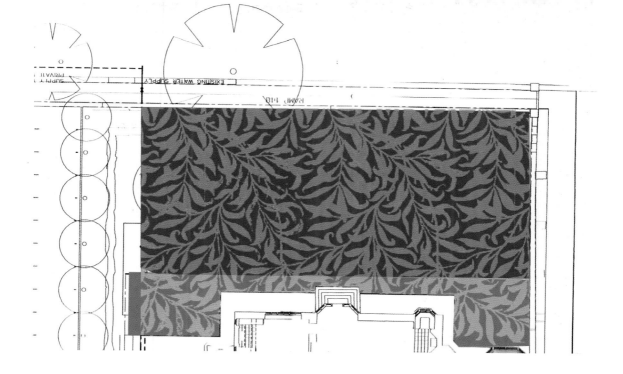

Artist Steve Messam specialises in site-specific installations. In the summer of 2010 he produced what he termed an 'environmental etching' for the lawns around Blackwell, an Arts and Crafts house in the English Lake District. 'LawnPaper' was based on the wallpaper designs of William Morris with their swirling patterns based on natural forms – leaves and flowers. This temporary intervention on the terraced lawn was made through a process of selective shading and trimming, the natural growth colouring the grass and giving a range of tones. It highlighted the central role that Morris played in the Arts and Crafts movement, as well as being true to its ideology. This kind of brief, transformatory artwork allows viewers to see both the garden and the house in a fresh way.

Some of Messam's work was achieved with a small, hand push mower. By adjusting mowing heights, and freeing the imagination from the usual up and down stripes, lawns can be transformed with temporary patterns. A vibrant series of lines can follow the edge of a border, leading the eye to a distant point, emphasising the fluidity of the land. The labyrinth, a single unbranching path (in contrast to the choice of paths in a maze) has long been used as an aid to meditation. Using a simple method of knotted string from a central point, a labyrinth can be cut into a lawn with the mower blades set at differing heights. Each year a different design can transform a plain lawn into a thoughtful, calming labyrinth to walk meditatively to its central point.

A chequerboard design in grass by Roberto Burle Marx, Brazil

Patterns cut by mower enliven this Welsh lawn

Grass is particularly easy to create patterns with. Small changes in height result in different hues, shadows and texture. There is something incredibly inviting in a short-cropped path leading into a meadow of long, waving grasses and wildflowers. The mown path clarifies the edges, makes it look well cared for and deliberate and leads the eye into the picture. In a lawn space all kinds of patterns can be constructed by having fun with the process of mowing; chequerboards of squares, grids with triangles, circles or freely snaking shapes. By winter the design is lost to be reborn as something new in the next season.

Guerrilla gardening

The way that gardens can be so easily swept away is what makes them so poignant. Development, garden grabbing, change of ownership or weather events can all so easily destroy what it can take years to perfect. This gives them a beauty like that of a butterfly, appreciated for the time that they exist. Taking an unloved urban space and changing it just for a brief period into something colourful and rewarding is the work of guerrilla gardeners. The term was first used in 1973 in New York when Liz Christy and a group of gardening activists called themselves the Green Guerrillas. Finding inaccessible, derelict plots they would hurl 'seed bombs' containing soil, seeds and fertiliser to cover the site.

A more permanent garden bears her name. The Liz Christy Community Garden, rented from the City since 1974, is a thriving space transformed from what used to be a garbage and rubble covered plot on the northeast corner of Bowery and Houston Streets in Manhattan. Wildlife abounds where once all was ugliness and dereliction; there are trees, herbs, vegetables, flowers, grapevines and places to sit, a true refuge in the city. Community gardens bring together people of all ages and races, have benefits for physical and mental health and bring respect and care for the environment. But there is still much neglect and ugliness in our cities and it is this that guerrilla gardeners, often illicitly, act to counter.

The Liz Christy Community Garden
in New York City

There are guerrilla gardening groups all over the world, their set-up and communication made easier thanks to the social media. Richard Reynolds, a London-based activist, has his own website and has written a book about projects carried out in 30 different countries. People post before and after photographs of the actions large and small that they undertake across the world. They range from the size of one paving slab on a sidewalk to large abandoned plots. Urban authorities vary in their attitudes to these activities, and some spaces that are targeted are on busy traffic islands, so guerrilla gardening may be carried out at night.

Generally more accepted these days, one of Richard Reynolds' projects involved planting a London roundabout with tulips for spring and lavender bushes for summer flowering. The lavender is then harvested and made into scented pillows that are sold to help fund further work. In 2011 HRH The Duchess of Cornwall, like the Prince of Wales a keen gardener, joined in the lavender harvest (with the approval of the site owners).

Guerrilla gardening is a spontaneous response to unsightly, unused urban spaces but by its nature usually only has a brief lifespan. The flowers that germinate from seed bombs brighten wasteland with their temporary colour. Plots are used for growing before the land is built on. Traffic islands are made into gardens and bring fleeting pleasure to commuters. Any garden is subject to change or may be lost but the temporary pleasure that these interventions bring is a celebration of the joy of growing things.

ABOVE
The Duchess of Cornwall helping guerrilla gardener Richard Reynolds harvest lavender in London

LEFT
Plants bedeck an old boombox

Anything can be used to hold plants - even this blue chest of drawers

Recycling

Cottage gardeners the world over have always used whatever came to hand as containers for growing plants: drainpipes, baskets, colanders, mugs, trunks, tin baths, teapots, wheelbarrows and all manner of household items. Add to these ladders as ledges for plants, suitcases spilling out flowers, trainers, jugs, teapots, boats or even old cars. Olive oil tins in the Mediterranean seem especially appropriate for growing basil and other herbs. Then there are old work boots filled with sedums nailed to fence posts, bricks with holes in them just the right size for drought resistant houseleeks, watering cans that no longer hold water but that are perfect for growing strawberries. Way before the word 'recycling' was in common usage, this was a way of not wasting anything and putting a bit of joy into gardening at the same time.

A fence made from an eclectic mix of old tools

Utilising things that might otherwise be thrown away is spontaneous and unselfconscious and therein lies its charm. It is from the same root that folk art enters gardens, a personal need for expression that is unsophisticated and instinctive. Garden buildings may be adorned with shells or pebbles, mosaics made from broken crockery, walls constructed with the blue and green bases of wine bottles. Once begun, they can become obsessive, with more and more elements being added to the creation.

Themed gardens

Gardens can also be created around a theme. This gives a focus to the design and can be educational, inspirational and atmospheric. The Alnwick Poison Garden in northern England consists of plants which can be deadly if ingested and fascinates and thrills its visitors. The garden contains over 100 different plants; some are beautiful as well as dangerous. Perhaps a macabre theme to choose but fascinating in its own way. With its locked gates, storytelling guides and grisly tales it uses drama and imagery to relate legends and facts about plants.

A themed garden can recreate a historical period; this might be a Roman garden, Elizabethan garden or a frontier settler's garden. One of the finest Roman gardens outside Italy can be found in north Portugal at the ruined town of Conimbriga. Here amongst magnificent bathhouses, heating systems and mosaics, is a replanted garden set within the colonnaded courtyard. Irises grow in raised, curved beds made of brick, formally laid out in a pool that spouts jets of water. There is something nostalgic and comforting about gardens that emulate the past. In America there is a great fondness for frontier gardens with their white picket fences, herbs, flowers and vegetables grown for self-sufficiency and for pleasure.

Roman garden at the Getty Villa, Malibu, California

A grand theme is behind the World Garden at Lullingstone Castle in Kent, England. Laid out in the shape of a map of the world, plants are positioned according to their country of origin. This celebrates the work of those intrepid plant hunters who risked life to seek out and bring back new specimens. Its creator, Tom Hart Dyke, did indeed risk his life searching for orchids in the Darien Gap between North and South America. Kidnapped by Colombian guerrillas, Tom spent nine months of captivity designing his dream garden for his family home. Once released, he planted the castle garden with a staggering 8,000 species of plants.

Themed gardens can reflect the monastic tradition, focus on herbs and healing, or celebrate Shakespeare's plants, as in Central Park, New York. A garden can be a narrative, telling a story, bringing individuality and identity.

Unique gardens

There is a unique garden in north Northumberland close to the border between England and Scotland and a short distance from the sixteenth century battle site of Flodden Field. The Cement Menagerie in the village of Branxton crams about 300 sculptures, mainly of animals, amongst perennials, clipped shrubs and garden ponds. It is a strange experience to wander round twisting paths and encounter Churchill puffing on his cigar, a giraffe towering above you, a flock of sheep or Lawrence of Arabia on his camel. This idiosyncratic collection was begun in 1962 by John Fairington, an 80-year-old joiner, to amuse his son who had cerebral palsy. Together with James Beveridge, of similar pensionable age, he moulded the cement over iron and wire netting before painting it in bright colours. Like the best unselfconscious, quirky gardens, it was made for purely private pleasure, a very personal creation and delightful as a result.

Possibly the most outlandish garden of all is the Bosco Sacro (sacred grove) at Bomarzo. This sixteenth century Italian park, also known as the Parco dei Mostri or grove of monsters, was created by Pier Francesco Orsini after the death of his wife. Fanciful and unsettling, the huge sculptures, many carved from living rock, loom out of the woodland, their stone surfaces greened with moss and algae, their symbolism obscure, their effect haunting. A house leans at a surreal angle, one of Hannibal's war elephants mauls a Roman legionary, a giant tears apart his upturned enemy. A space is carved within the screaming mouth of a giant mask with flaring nostrils. Bomarzo is the height of the bizarre. It is melancholy and strange, and utterly unique.

Folk art in the Cement Menagerie, Branxton, England

The yawning mouth at the entrance to Bomarzo, Italy

This drive to create something unconventional has motivated some surprising gardens, often by artist-gardeners. The French artist Niki de Saint Phalle began work in 1979 on a garden in Tuscany that she based on the major arcana of tarot cards. Her 22 monumental sculptures in bright colours create a fantasy world of huge, often female figures, covered in mosaics, mirrors and paint, some so large that there were rooms inside. Whilst she was making the garden, Niki de Saint Phalle actually lived in the Empress figure. The garden is an exploration of her experience of the world, in particular of what it is to be a woman. Such extraordinary gardens cannot be neatly slotted into a particular art movement or garden style, born as they are from the imagination and conviction of one person. It is this realization of the capricious and idiosyncratic that brings an extra dimension to artful gardening. Whether it

be an entire fantasy garden or a small detail of whimsy, it has the ability to make us think, to amuse, to frighten or to bring more richness to our lives.

Gardening brings that richness to our lives and it appeals on so many different levels. Artful garden design uses those elements that often inform artworks – colour, texture, composition and all the other terms so familiar to artists and gardeners alike. Experience and skill give depth to how we go about making gardens, but a key quality is to have sensitivity to that which is being created, to the raw materials and plants that are being used. The inspiring photographs in this book are the jumping off points for your own discoveries and experimentation. Take joy and delight in looking at and making gardens and the rest will naturally follow.

Niki de Saint Phalle's extraordinary garden

CHECKLISTS

CHECKLISTS

PRINCIPLE 1:
COMPOSITION

1. Prepare a large flat sheet of paper on which you can draw your garden plan or use an online garden template available from various companies.

2. Think about how you would walk through the space and try to imagine it in three-dimensions.

3. Will the garden be one large space or will you have small special areas as well?

4. What will be the fixed point for the garden?

5. Will your garden be formal or informal?

6. Thinking about your house, is it ultra modern or traditional? Gardens work best when they reflect the architecture of the building.

7. Is there a particular view that you want to highlight?

PRINCIPLE 2:
SIZE AND SCALE

1. How large a space will your garden fill?

2. Have you thought about the vertical aspect of your garden? If it is small creating vertical lines with trees or pergolas will draw the eye upwards.

3. Would adding a mirror in the garden help create the illusion of more space?

4. Are there ways you can alter the perspective by placing larger elements in the front and smaller ones at a distance or vice versa?

5. Are all the elements in your garden in proportion? For example, is the size of the paving stones appropriate or are they too large for the area they will cover?

6. Think about the size of plants you want in your garden. Do you want small, delicate plants or tall majestic ones? How do you think these would change the way you perceive your place in the garden?

PRINCIPLE 3:
LINE, PATTERN AND SHAPE

1. When thinking about a path, do you want to lead the eye directly to a focal point using straight lines or to create a journey with hidden surprises?

2. Can you play with the perspective by narrowing the path to give the illusion of a larger garden?

3. If you have decided on a classic formal garden, how will the line and pattern be laid out geometrically?

4. With an informal garden, if you want to guide the viewer gently around the garden will you use curved lines or straight lines softened by plantings?

5. Create a pattern in your garden by repeating colours and shapes or use a mass planting of a single species of plant to create a mood.

6. Could you use coloured sands or gravel to enhance the sense of pattern in the garden?

7. Bedding plants can be used to create intricate patterns that can be used on elevated banks or along borders.

8. Topiary can add both shape and pattern to a garden, especially valuable in winter.

PRINCIPLE 4:
LIGHT

1. Is your garden primarily north facing or south facing?

2. Have you looked at the space for your garden at different times of day to see how the light falls across it?

3. In a hotter climate, do you want to create places where you are shaded from the sun?

4. In a northerly climate, you want to draw in as much light as possible.

5. Is there a view of either sunrise or sunset that you want to frame?

6. The shadows of trees can create lovely effects, as can topiary shapes.

7. Artificial light at night can create magical visual effects, is there an area that could be transformed with the right placement of lights?

PICTURE CREDITS

Every effort has been made to credit the appropriate source. If there have been any errors or omissions, please contact us and we will undertake to make any corrections in the next printing.

© Tom White, pp 9, 25, 53, 70 (bottom), 76 (top and bottom); Julieanne Porter, Oxford Sow & Grow, p 10; courtesy Richard Tulloch.wordpress.com, p 17; courtesy Lou (*I descend from Vikings* blog 24/03/2010), p 43 (left); courtesy © Evelyn Williams 2012, p 52; © Simon Fraser, p 58; courtesy © Nature & Cities wallpapers (globeattractions.com), p 59; © Chris Parsons, p 152; © Steve Messam, p 153; © Laura Goggin, p 155; © Mark Holsworth, p 156;

All from **GAP Photos** ©: Elke Borkowski, pp 6, 50, 69, 80, 110, 134 (bottom); Jonathan Buckley, p 11, 95 (top right); Ron Evans, p 13; Abigail Rex, p 14; Jerry Harpur/Design: William Robinson, p 15; Hanneke Reijbroek/Design: Mien Ruys garden/Holland, pp 16, 52 (top left); Andrea Jones/Design: Oehme, van Sweden Associates, p 19; Carole Drake/courtesy of Mr & Mrs N Elliott, p 20; Jerry Harpur/Design: Sam Martin, p 22; Carole Drake, pp 26, 48, 52 (bottom left), 79 (bottom); Jerry Harpur, pp 28, 86 (left), 103 (right), 112, 149 (top), 151 (left); Jerry Harpur/Design: Topher Delaney, pp 29, 150 (right); Jerry Harpur/Design: Isabelle C Greene, p 30; Graham Strong, p 31; Jerry Harpur/Design: Steve Martino, pp 32, 81, 149 (bottom); Jerry Harpur/Design: Shunmayo Masuno, pp 34, 35, 133; Paul Debois/Design: Caroline De Lane Lea and Louise Cummins, p 36; Jerry Harpur/Design: Roja Dove, p 39; Suzie Gibbons/Design: Veronica Clein, p 40; Robert Mabic, p 41 (left); J S Sira, pp 41 (right), 56 (top); Nicola Browne/Design: Bernard Hicks, p 42; Jerry Harpur/ Design: Topher Delaney Oliver, p 43; Friedrich Strauss, p 44; Christa Brand, p 45; Victoria Firmston, p 46; Leigh Clapp, p 49; Andrea Jones, p 51 (left); Richard Bloom/Design: Dennis Schrader and Bill Smith, p 51 (right); Juliette Wade, p 54 (top); Charles Hawes, p 54 (bottom), 109, 154 (bottom); John Glover, pp 55 (top left), 93 (top right), 100; Ron Evans, p 55 (top right); FhF Greenmedia, p 55 (bottom right), 117, 140 (right), 148 (top); Jerry Harpur/Design: William Robinson, p 56 (bottom); Carole Drake/courtesy Bourton House, p 60; Charles Hawes, pp 62, 87; Andrea Jones/Design: Doug Reed of Reed Hilderbrand Associates, p 65; Lynn Keddie, p 66; Jo Whitworth, p 67, 68; Howard Rice, p 70 (top); Clive Nichols/ Designer: Charlotte Rowe, p 71; Jan Smith, p 72; Fiona McLeod, p 74; Clive Nichols, pp 77, 92 (bottom); Neil Holmes/Designer: Piet Oudolf, p 79 (top); Simon Colmer, p 82; Mark Bolton, pp 83, 124; Jerry Harpur/Design: Fernando Caruncho, p 84; Jenny Lilly, p 85; Julie Dansereau/Design: Patrick Blanc, p 86 (right); Jonathan Buckley/Design: Sarah Raven, Perch Hill, p 88; S & O, p 90; Heather Edwards/Design: Sim Flemons and John Warland, p 92 (top); Christina Bollen, p 93 (left); BBC Magazines Ltd, p 93 (bottom right); Christa Brand, p 94; Richard Bloom, p 95 (top left); Marcus Harpur/ Design: Nicky Baker, p 95 (bottom left); Heather Edwards, p 96;

Nadia MacKenzie/Design: Jonathan Denby and Philippa Pearson, p 98; Carole Drake/courtesy of Mr Nick Priestland, p 102; Paul Debois, p 103 (left); Jerry Harpur/Design: Jaques Wirtz, p 104; Fiona Lea, p 105 (top), 107 (right), 158; Andrea Jones/Design: James Alexander-Sinclair, p 105 (bottom); John Glover/Design: Alan Gardener, p 106; Charles Hawes/Design: Merrist Wood College, p 107 (left); Matt Anker, pp 108, 139; Howard Rice, p 114; Rob Whitworth, p 115; Jerry Harpur/Design: Isabelle C Green, p 116; Abigail Rex, p 118; Andrea Jones/Design: Luciana Giubbilei, p 119; Lynn Keddie, p 121; Claire Takacs, p 122 (top); Stephen Studd, p 122 (bottom); Jonathan Buckley/Design: Christopher Lloyd, p 126 (left), 127 (left), 127 (right); Jason Smalley, p 126 (right); Leigh Clapp, p 128; Jerry Harpur/Design: Marcus Barnett and Philip Nixon, p 130; Jenny Lilly, p 132; Leigh Clapp/Design: Yiva Blid-Mackenzie, p 134 (top); Heather Edwards/Design: Nick Williams-Ellis, p 136; Jerry Harpur/Design: Michael van Valkenburgh Associates, p 137; Clive Nichols/Festival de Jardins, Chaumont-Sur-Loire Design: Andy Cao and Stephen Jerrom, p 138; Richard Bloom, p 140 (left); Paul Debois/Design: Paul Stone, p 141; Juliette Wade/Roger Gladwell Landscapes, p 142; Jerry Harpur/Design: Stephen Stimson, p 144; Richard Bloom, p 147; Jerry Harpur/Design Ulf Nordfjell, p 148 (bottom); Jerry Harpur/Design: Pamela Burton, p 150 (left); Howard Rice, p 151 (right); Jerry Harpur/Design: Roberto Burle Marx/Gilbert Strunk, p 154 (top); Charles Hawes, p 154 (bottom), 164; Paul Debois, p 157; Carole Drake/courtesy Ian Willis, p 159; Rachel Warne, p 160; Marion Brenner/Roger Warner Design, p 161

ACKNOWLEDGMENTS

It was wonderful to be able to pay tribute to some of my gardening heroes in this book, as well as to discover new sources of inspiration. Thanks, therefore, go to Vivays Publishing for thinking of its title and to Lee Ripley in particular for her skill and advice.

I'd like to thank the designers of these remarkable gardens and the photographers who have captured them so brilliantly. Their work encompasses two forms of art; firstly in the creation of these extraordinary spaces, then through the vision of the photographer.

And many thanks go to my garden designer daughter Emma White who is working on a PhD on the restorative qualities of gardens. To have someone so well qualified to read the text gave me great confidence.